Lifelines 3

COPING SKILLS IN ENGLISH

SECOND EDITION

Barbara Foley

Howard Pomann

Institute for Intensive English
Union County College, New Jersey

PRENTICE HALL REGENTS

Acquisitions editor: Nancy Leonhardt
Production supervision: Noël Vreeland Carter
Interior design: A Good Thing and Jerry Vota
Cover design: Jerry Vota
Illustrations: Don Martinetti, D.M. Graphics, Inc.
Manufacturing Buyer and Scheduler: Ray Keating

Photo Credits:
Laima Druskis, Units 1, 3, and 10, page 59; Ken Karp, Units 2, 7, and 10, page 56; Rhoda Sidney
Units 4 and 11; Birmingham View Co., Birmingham, Alabama, Unit 6; National Institutes of
Health, Unit 8; Larry Flemming, Unit 9; Paige Poore, Unit 10, page 59; Irene Springer, Unit 13;
A.T.& T. Co., Photo Center, Unit 15.

Printed in the United States of America
20 19 18 17 16 15 14 13 12 11

ISBN 0-13-225574-X

This series is dedicated to our dear friend and colleague, Gretchen Dowling
Gretchen Dowling
8/31/43–4/13/89

Contents

Introduction

Barbara Foley and Howard Pomann have devised this survival skills series specifically for entry-level adult students who need to learn basic skills and basic language in order to function effectively in the United States. The Conversations and practices lead students through carefully controlled exercises to the point where they can "put it together" for themselves. In addition to whole-class and large-group activities, LIFELINES features many small-group activities which allow the teacher to step aside and became a facilitator as the students work together using the language in new and different ways. The focus on coping skills and functional language, rather than grammar and vocabulary, promotes learning by increasing student interest. The repetition of the same basic exercise formats throughout, allows students to concentrate on learning language, not exercise formats. Gretchen Dowling's excellent "To the Teacher" section gives clear explanations of how to do each exercise, along with an abundance of ideas for adapting them to your own individuals needs. Photographs, drawings and realia bring the content of each unit to life for students. LIFELINES really makes learning easier for your students, and teaching easier for you.

Sharon Seymour
Alemany Community
College Center
San Francisco

To the Teacher

LIFELINES is a four-book ESL coping skills series for adult learners at entry, beginning, low-intermediate and intermediate levels. Each book deals with ten or more different coping skill areas. The series is competency-based and integrates the coping skills with the essential language forms, vocabulary, and cultural information needed in each situation.

Skill areas are reintroduced throughout the series with different competencies. For example, in "Telephone," in Book 1, students ask to speak with someone; in Book 2, they leave a simple message; in Book 3, they give and take a longer message; in Book 4, they ask for the right person or office. Those competencies requiring simpler language forms come before those calling for more difficult ones. Thus, grammatical points such as verb tenses are introduced in appropriate sequence. They are reintroduced cyclically throughout the series and via the different contexts within each book.

The series is suitable for a wide variety of adult and secondary school classes. It could be the total program, for example, for open-entry ESL classes of 3-6 hours per week. For intensive language courses, it would be one strand of the total program. In community college or secondary school classes, it could be used either to reinforce grammatical structures, or to introduce them in context.

Each unit is self-contained, takes approximately two hours, and affords practice in listening, speaking, reading, and writing. The table of contents for each book lists the coping skill areas, the functions or competencies, and the main grammatical structures in each chapter. This gives the teacher easy access to the information needed to choose how best to integrate LIFELINES with individual programs, classes, and teaching styles.

This series incorporates both whole class and small group learning activities. All the activities are designed to give students as much "inner space" as possible to process the language according to their own individual learning styles. Those for the whole class are to introduce or sum up the structure, vocabulary, and cultural information needed to perform the coping skill; those for the small groups, to provide students with the intensive independent practice they need to make the language their own.

In the whole class activities, the teacher utilizes stories, pictures, and conversations to introduce the new language and information in the chapter. Although the teacher is leading the activity, the activities are designed so that the teacher can easily elicit the correct language with minimal teacher modeling.

In smaller group activities, the teacher's role is that of a small group facilitator assisting the students in completing their tasks, rather than of a leader. Depending on the activity and level of the students, a teacher can circulate from group to group, stay with one group, or sit separately from the groups and assist only when asked.

Students working in small groups learn to discover their own mistakes, to correct each other, to share opinions, to experiment with the language, and to work as a learning community. Small groups allow the teacher to divide the class according to particular language needs, and to work with students having individual problems as well as those who are ahead of the class. They also free students to ask questions they may not ask in the whole class setting.

For the teacher, one of the biggest advantages of LIFELINES is that small group work, and accommodation to different learning styles, are built-in. It is not necessary to supplement the books with small group tasks in order to meet individual student needs. The small group activities have been tested with a wide variety of students. They work without extra work for the teacher.

Naturally, there are many ways to handle the activities presented in the workbooks, depending on students' proficiency levels, and the teacher's personal style. In the pages which follow, the authors offer "how to" suggestions which have proven effective for them. These are intended simply as some ways to structure classwork so that students have maximum opportunity to meet their own learning needs in a productive and secure atmosphere. They are not intended as limits on the readers' style or creativity.

WHOLE CLASS ACTIVITIES

Discuss

Discuss
The Discuss questions and accompanying illustration or photo set the scene for the unit. The class should talk about the illustration and what they see happening in the picture. The Discuss questions help the student to relate their personal opinions and experiences to the theme of the unit. Cultural comments and explanations can be made at this time. During this introduction to the unit, the focus is on expanding the students' knowledge of the coping skill rather than the correction of grammar.

Read

Read
A short factual reading introduces the main cultural theme of each of each unit. Students read the story silently twice. In the first reading, students should concentrate on the general ideas of the passage and not try to understand every word or to analyze the structures. During the second reading, students should concentrate on understanding and interpreting the materials. After the students finish reading, they complete the true/false exercise which focuses on the main ideas and supporting details. Once this exercise is completed, the class discusses the new vocabulary, clarifies the main concepts, and expands on the content.

Listen, Read and Say

Listen, Read and Say
This is the dialogue which introduces the language and competency. It is the core from which all the other activities and expansions in the chapter emerge. Thus, it is vital that the meaning be clear to the students.

Step 1: Students read the dialogue to themselves and figure out as much of the meaning as they can on their own. During this process, they can talk to each other and even translate. The surer they are that they know what the dialogue says in their own language, the easier it is for them to "let go" and absorb the English. The teacher can circulate, answering individual questions and/or getting a sense of what may be needed to explain to the entire group.

Step 2: When students feel reasonably clear about the meaning, the teacher makes any necessary further clarification, dramatizations, or explanations. The teacher may then want to read the dialogue aloud once or twice while students listen and look at their books. This helps them associate the sound of English with the meanings they have worked out. The dialogue may be written on the board and the students asked to close their books. This serves as a signal to focus on English together.

Step 3: Practice the dialogue. (a) This can be done by the usual choral then individual repetition, followed by half the class taking in speaker's part while half takes the other, culminating with individual students role playing the parts.

(b) A variation or supplement to this is to change the "rules of the game" and have the teacher repeat after the students. The teacher stands at the back of the room, and lets the students, one at a time, call out whatever word, phrase or sentence they want to hear. The teacher repeats the student's utterance until the student stops initiating the repetition. The teacher behaves like a tape recorder with a natural, non-judgmental voice: by just letting the students hear the utterance they "ask" for, the exercise helps them self-correct and develop their own criteria for grammar and pronunciation. If students fail to self-correct an important point, it is best to deal with the point after the exercise, rather than to break the mood of the self-directed learning.

Since this exercise is a bit different from what most classes are accustomed to, it is necessary to explain it clearly beforehand. With very basic classes to whom one cannot translate, it often helps to number the sentences in the dialogue. Then the teacher can say and easily demonstrate, "Tell me the number you want to hear. I will say the sentence. If you say the number again, I will repeat the sentence. I am a machine. I will repeat what you say. I will stop when you say 'stop'."

(c) As an aid to internalizing the dialogue, the teacher can erase every fifth word and replace it with a line, having students read the dialogue while orally filling in the missing words. This procedure is repeated with lines for every third word, and so on, until students are "reading" a dialogue composed of completely blank lines. Members of the class might then cooperate in filling in all the blanks to reinforce correct spelling, etc.

Practice

This activity introduces new vocabulary within the previously established context and grammatical structures. A single sentence or interaction from the dialogue is given as the model. Students practice the model, substituting the vocabulary cued by the pictures below it.

Step 1: If much of the vocabulary is new, students can repeat each item in isolation, chorally and then individually, following the teacher's model.

Step 2: The teacher elicits the use of the new items within the model sentence or interaction. One way to do this is simply to have the students repeat the complete utterances after the teacher. This is a good first step, especially for very low-level classes. After this initial security is given, however, students need a little more independence.

A variation, or follow-up, is for the teacher to give only the first utterance as a model. The teacher then simply points to or calls out the number of each different picture and has the students give the complete utterance. This can be done both chorally and individually.

Step 3: Students can then continue practicing all the substitutions, with the person sitting next to them. The teacher can circulate, helping with pronunciation as necessary.

Step 4: To further reinforce the pronunciation of the new vocabulary, follow the procedures described in Step 4b of Listen, Read, and Say.

SMALL GROUP ACTIVITIES

Before beginning the small group activities, the teacher divides the students in groups of two to five depending on the activity and the size of the class. The teacher then goes over the directions carefully and demonstrates what each student will do, explaining what the teacher's role will be, whether circulating from group to group, or staying with one group. The teacher should give the students a time frame; for example, telling the students they have fifteen minutes to complete the task. The time frame can always be extended. Clear information about what to expect helps students feel secure and be more productive.

There are many different ways to group students. Some teachers like to have students of the same ability together; others to mix them so the more advanced can help the slower. Some like to mix language backgrounds in order to encourage the use of English; other have the same backgrounds together in order to raise the security level, or to facilitate students' explaining things to each other. Some like student self-selection so that working friendships may develop more easily; others don't see this as crucial to the development of supportive, productive groups. Each teacher's values and pedagogical purposes will determine the way the class is divided into groups.

Partner Exercise

Partner Exercise

This small-group activity is designed for two students to practice a specific grammatical structure in a controlled interaction. The left-hand column of the *Partner Exercise* gives word or picture cues from which Student 1 forms a statement or question. The right-hand column gives the complete sentences. Student 2 looks at this column, using it to be "teacher" and check the utterances of the other student. Students are to fold the page in the middle so that S1 is looking at the left-hand column and S2 at the right.

Step 1: The teacher explains all this to the students. One way is to copy two or three items in the left-hand column on one side of the board. (It is not necessary to worry about awkward picture drawing; it usually just provides a few moments of laughter for the class.)

(b) Then draw the corresponding items from the right-hand column on the other side of the board.

(c) The teacher assumes the roles of the two students and demonstrates what each is to do.

(d) The teacher calls for student volunteers to come to come up to the board, stand in front of the appropriate columns, and do the exercise.

(e) The teacher demonstrates folding the exercise page, and indicates which side each is to look at.

Step 2: Students form into pairs of students.

Step 3: Students fold their pages and do the exercise.

Step 4: The teacher can circulate from group to group assisting when asked or needed, encouraging students to listen carefully and to correct each other's sentences and pronunciation.

Step 5: When a pair has completed the exercise, the two students should change roles and do it again.

Complete

Completion activities provide writing practice and the use of individual cognitive skills. Students are asked, for example, to complete sentences, write questions, fill in forms, find and apply information from charts or maps, etc. Directions are specific for each activity. To explain and structure the activities, the teacher can use the chalkboard. As the students write individually or in small groups, the teacher circulates, giving assistance as needed or requested.

Interaction

The Interaction Charts give the students a structured opportunity to practice their new language with one or two other students. Each activity begins with two or more questions about the topic.

Step 1: Students sit with a partner and ask each question. They mark their partner's response on the chart, usually by recording a "yes" or "no," circling an appropriate response or writing a single word. The students then switch roles. Often, other language and questions emerge as the students interact. The teacher should encourage the students to speak freely and gain confidence in their language use.

Step 2: Repeat Step 1 with a different partner. Most interaction charts ask the students to speck with two students.

Step 3: After the students have their partners' responses, several students should report their information back to the class. Typically, the teacher will ask a student, "Who(m) did you speak to?" and "What did he tell you?" The goal in this activity is correctly reporting information and using the new vocabulary. Do not focus on the correctness of the grammar.

Putting It Together

The last two pages in each unit give the students the opportunity to practice and expand the coping and language skills emphasized in the units' more open-ended conversation. In most chapters, a problem solving situation is introduced with a short reading and a detailed illustration. As a whole class or in small groups, students read the problem aloud, discuss the picture, and answer a series of questions to become familiar with the situation and the issues surrounding it. Students then have the opportunity to discuss their opinions and suggest solutions to resolve the problem through various small group discussion and writing activities.

Role Play

A Role Play or Go Find Out is the final activity. With a role play, the students work together as partners and write a conversation about the coping skill area. The students have the support of the previous activities to help create the dialogue. The teacher circulates, giving assistance as needed and requested. The students practice the conversations without looking at their papers, and then stand in front of the class and act out their conversations. Whenever this kind of freedom is given, a teacher may expect less perfection in students language than during controlled practice.

Go Find Out

Find out In the Go Find Out students are asked to find out specific information about services, agencies or businesses in their communities. For the next class, students report their findings to the other students.

Gretchen Dowling
Barbara H. Foley
Howard Pomann

Acknowledgments

The development of this series has been the result of a long growth process. We wish to thank our many friends and colleagues who have given their support, shared their ideas, and increased our insights into the language-learning process and its application in the ESL classroom:

John Chapman, Ralph Colognori, Joyce Ann Custer, Mary Dolan, John Duffy, Jacqueline Flamm, Irene Frankel, Susan Lanzano, Joann LaPerla, Darlene Larson, Nancy Liggera, Fred Malkemes, Joy Noren, Douglas Pillsbury, Deborah Pires, Sherri Preiss, Jennybelle Rardin, Sharon Seymour, Earl Stevick, and the Westfield Police Department, and the faculty at the Institute for Intensive English, Union College.

A special thanks go to our parents, Muriel and Warren Haedrich and Evelyn and Julius Pomann for their encouragement and love.

Barbara Foley
Howard Pomann

1 What's New?

Discuss

What's new with you?
What's new with your family?
What do you talk about when you see a
    friend or a neighbor?

Read

When Americans meet their friends, they often begin their conversations with a greeting and then ask about the friend's health, family, or job. Most of the time these conversations are short and about happy events. People discuss special family occasions such as marriages, births, graduations, new jobs, new homes, and vacations. One friend will usually wish the other good luck or offer congratulations. People also talk about unhappy events, such as a serious illness, accident, or death. Friends express sympathy and often ask if they can help. Americans don't talk about personal family problems with casual friends.

It is not easy to meet and talk to neighbors. In the United States neighbors are usually polite and sometimes become friends. Usually neighbors know each others' names and are acquaintances. When neighbors meet, they wave, say "Hello" or "How are you?", and continue on with their business for the day. Neighbors may get to know one another better and may become friends if they have young children, dogs, gardens, or similar interests.

Read each sentence. If it is true, write T. If it is false, write F.

_____ 1. Friends sometimes discuss sad events.

_____ 2. When Americans meet a friend on the street, they often talk for five minutes or more.

_____ 3. When friends meet, it is polite to ask about marriage problems.

_____ 4. Most Americans are good friends with their neighbors.

_____ 5. Neighbors usually stop and have a conversation when they see each other in the morning.

Luis: Hi, Magda. How are you?
Magda: Not bad. How about you?
Luis: Good. How are your parents? I haven't seen them for a while.
Magda: They're really busy. They just sold their house and they're moving to Florida.
Luis: That's great. You can visit them in the winter.
Magda: Yes. They have an extra bedroom. We'll probably fly down there in December.
Luis: Say "Hi" to them for me.
Magda: I will.

Practice this model with the pictures below.

A: How _____*are*_____ your _____*parents*_____?
B: _____*They*_____ just *sold their house* and *they're moving to Florida.*

1. your parents
   sell their house
   move to Florida

2. your sister
   have a baby
   come home tomorrow

3. your son
   get married
   look for an apartment

4. you
   get laid off
   look for a new job

3

Practice this model with the pictures below.

> A: What's new with your ___children___ ?
> B: ___My daughter___ just ___finished college___ and
>   ___my son is working in a bank.___

1. children
   My daughter / finish college   and   my son / work in a bank

2. children
   My son / graduate from high school   and   my daughter / go to college

3. parents
   My father / pass away   and   my mother / live with us

4. parents
   My father / retire   and   my mother / work in an office

Partner Exercise

Talk about these family members.

Student 1

father/retire/move to Florida
My father just retired and he's moving to Florida.

1. father/retire/move to Florida
2. husband/have an operation/come home soon
3. brother/sell his house/look for an apartment
4. sister/finish nursing school/work in a hospital

5. father/have a heart attack/recover at home
6. wife/get laid off/look for a new job
7. daughter/get divorced/move back home

(FOLD HERE)

Student 2
Listen carefully and help Student 1.

1. My father just retired and he's moving to Florida.
2. My husband just had an operation and he's coming home soon.
3. My brother just sold his house and he's looking for an apartment.
4. My sister just finished nursing school and she's working in a hospital.
5. My father just had a heart attack and he's recovering at home.
6. My wife just got laid off and she's looking for a new job.
7. My daughter just got divorced and she's moving back home.

Repeat these responses after the teacher. Talk about when to use each one. Then, read the situations below and decide which responses are appropriate. Write one choice on the line next to the sentence.

That's great!
That's wonderful!
I'm happy to hear that.
Congratulations.
Good luck.

That's terrible.
That's awful.
That's too bad.
That's a shame.
I'm sorry to hear that.

1. I just got a promotion.   _____**Congratulations.**_____

2. I just got laid off.   _____

3. My brother just got married.   _____

4. My sister just got divorced.   _____

5. My son just graduated from high school.   _____

6. My mother just passed away.   _____

7. My father just had a heart attack.   _____

8. My parents just celebrated their twenty-fifth wedding anniversary.   _____

5

Complete these sentences about a family. Add an appropriate response.

1. John: What's new?

    Lisa: I just _____ (find) a new job and I _____ (start)

             tomorrow.

    John: _____.

2. Joseph: How are your parents?

    Pierre: Great! They just _____ (celebrate) their fortieth wedding

             anniversary and they _____ (take) a vacation in Hawaii.

    Joseph: _____.

3. Sarah: How's your son?

    Betty: He just _____ (graduate) from high school and he

             _____ (go) into the navy.

    Sarah: _____.

4. Hannah: How's your brother?

    Gloria: Not too well. He just _____ (have) another operation

             and he _____ (feel) very depressed.

    Hannah: _____.

Interaction

Ask two students about themselves and their families. Fill in their answers on the chart below.

QUESTION	STUDENT 1	STUDENT 2
What's new with you?		
What's new with your family?		

Role play

With another student, write and practice a conversation between two friends who have not seen one another for a month or two. Ask about different family members. Present your dialogue to the class.

6

John met Luis at the store yesterday. John was surprised to hear that Luis lost his job at the auto parts company about three months ago. Luis is married and has a one-year-old child. His wife, Elena, works part time in the evening. Luis and Elena are having trouble making ends meet. Elena's parents live in the same town and have an extra bedroom in their apartment. They have asked them to move in. Luis and Elena are trying to decide what to do.

Discuss these questions.

1. What's new with Luis and Elena?
2. How does Luis feel?
3. What will happen if they can't pay their rent?
4. What would you say to Luis if you met him?
5. Why is Elena working only part time?
6. Should they stay in their apartment or move in with Elena's parents?
7. Should Elena look for a full-time job, too?
8. Should they consider moving to another city or state to find a job?
9. What do you think Luis and Elena should do? Write your opinion below. Share your opinion with the other students.

_____

_____

_____

_____

2 School

Discuss

Do you have any children in school? What grades are they in?

How much homework do your children receive each night?

Did you ever attend a parent–teacher conference?

Read

Parents can help their children do well in school. They have to make sure that their children go to school every day, complete their homework assignments and have good study habits.

Good attendance in school is important so that children can keep up with their classwork. Parents should not take children out of school unless they are sick. In class, students are expected to participate. You should encourage your children to raise their hands, ask and answer questions, take notes, and be active members of the class.

At home, children must have a quiet place to study. The room should have a table, good lighting, and no TV or any other distractions. Children get homework every day. Parents should ask their children about their homework: "What is your homework tonight?" and "Do you have any tests this week?" Parents should be sure the homework is complete.

Once or twice a year, schools schedule parent–teacher conferences. At the conference, the teacher tells the parents about their child's progress in school and makes suggestions on how their child can improve. Parents have an opportunity to ask questions and find out about what is happening in the class. If parents notice that their child is having difficulty on tests or has poor grades on a report card, they should call the school and make an appointment with a teacher or the principal. Teachers want and expect parents to come and speak with them. Many schools offer before- and after-school help in all subjects.

Read each sentence. If it is true, write T. If it is false, write F.

_____ 1. If a person is sick, it is acceptable to take a child out of school for one day to translate at the doctor's office.

_____ 2. Most American students raise their hands and actively participate when they know an answer.

_____ 3. Parents should know when their children are having tests.

_____ 4. If your child is a good student, it is not necessary to go to a parent–teacher conference.

_____ 5. You can make an appointment with the school principal to discuss your child's progress.

Mother:	Kevin got his report card today.
Father:	Let me see. How are his grades?
Mother:	Not bad. One A, three Bs, and a D.
Father:	Let me guess. The A is in math and the D is in French.
Mother:	Of course.
Father:	He does well in math. He's got a good head for numbers and he puts a lot of effort into it. But that's his second D in French.
Mother:	He does his homework, but he doesn't pass his tests. He says his teacher is boring.
Father:	That's his favorite excuse. Let's call his French teacher and set up a conference.

Practice this model and talk about schoolwork.

She	**participates in class.**

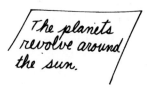

1. participate in class

2. do well in math

3. read well

4. work neatly and carefully

5. get along well with the other students

6. do his homework

Practice both models and talk about school problems.

| She | doesn't | *pay attention* | . |

| She | never | *pays attention* | . |

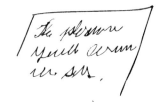

1. pay attention

2. do her homework

3. write neatly

4. understand the work

5. raise his hand

6. follow directions

**Partner
Exercise**

Talk about these students' class work.

Student 1
She/follow directions
She follows directions.

1. She / follow directions
2. He / talk all the time
3. She / not listen
4. He / complete his work on time
5. He / not do his homework
6. She / never raise her hand
7. She / communicate her ideas well
8. He / work independently
9. She / not contribute to class discussions
10. She / show effort
11. He / not write neatly
12. He / never ask for help

(FOLD HERE)

Student 2
Listen carefully and help Student 1.

1. She follows directions.
2. He talks all the time.
3. She doesn't listen.
4. He completes his work on time.
5. He doesn't do his homework.
6. She never raises her hand.
7. She communicates her ideas well.
8. He works independently.
9. She doesn't contribute to class discussions.
10. She shows effort.
11. He doesn't write neatly.
12. He never asks for help.

PUPIL PROGRESS REPORT

Grade 4

Name ___Carla Leonard___   Teacher ___Ms. Taylor___

MARKING CODE

A = Excellent Achievement	D = Work Meets Minimal Standards
B = Achievement of High Quality	F = Not Passing
C = Satisfactory Progress	* = Achievement, But Not at Grade Level

+ = Exceptional Progress
✓ = Additional Emphasis Needed

	1	2	3	4		1	2	3	4
READING	A				**SOCIAL STUDIES**	D			
Understands and uses new vocabulary	+				Applies reading and writing skills	+	✓		
Comprehends what is read					Understands basic concepts				
Reads independently	✓				Plans and completes projects	+	✓		
Completes assignments and homework					Understands maps, globes, and graphs	✓			
LANGUAGE	B				**SCIENCE**	C			
Communicates ideas orally					Understands basic concepts				
Communicates ideas in written work					Demonstrates achievement on tests				
Writes neatly	+				Understands vocabulary				
Completes assignments					Plans and completes projects	✓			
SPELLING	B				**SOCIAL ATTITUDES**	B			
Spells assigned words correctly					Works and plays well with others	✓			
Spells correctly in written work					Is dependable and responsible	+			
Completes homework	+				Respects school rules				
MATHEMATICS	B				Actively participates				
Understands concepts					**WORK HABITS**	A			
Computes with accuracy					Follows directions	+			
Able to solve word problems	✓				Works independently				
Knows the basic facts	✓	+			Requests help when needed				

Look at the report card carefully and complete these statements about Carla's schoolwork.

1. Carla _____*does*_____ (do) well in Reading.

2. In Reading, she _____*doesn't read*_____ (read) independently.

3. In Reading, she _____ (understand) the new vocabulary.

4. In Language, Carla _____ (write) neatly.

5. In Spelling, Carla _____ (complete) her homework.

6. In Math, she _____ (know) the basic facts well.

7. In Social Studies, she _____ (apply) her reading skills.

8. In Science, she _____ (complete) projects.

9. In Social Attitudes, Carla _____ (work) well with others.

10. In Work Habits, Carla _____ (follow) directions.

Michael, a student in seventh grade, came home today with a bad report card. His last report card was all Bs and Cs. On this report card, he had two Cs, two Ds, and one F. His parents don't know why his grades went down. Michael says that he doesn't like the teachers and that he gets too much homework.

Discuss these questions.

1. How old is Michael? What grade is he in?
2. Michael's grades went down. How do you think he feels?
3. How do you think his parents will react?
4. Where does Michael study?
5. Describe Michael's study habits. How can he improve them?
6. What are some other possible reasons for Michael's poor grades?
7. What do you think Michael's parents should do about his poor report card? Write your opinion below. Share your opinion with the other students.

_____

_____

_____

Sit in a small group. You are going to speak to Michael's teacher about his progress in French class. Write five questions you might ask the teacher. Share your questions with other groups.

1. _____

2. _____

3. _____

4. _____

5. _____

Interaction

Ask another student these questions about study habits. Fill in the chart below with information about your partner and about yourself.

QUESTIONS	YOUR PARTNER	YOU
Do you attend all your classes?		
Do you take notes in class?		
Do you copy examples and information that the teacher writes on the board?		
Do you ask questions if you don't understand the lesson?		
Do you do your homework?		
Do you schedule time to study?		
Do you study for tests?		
Do you ask the teacher for any class work if you are absent?		
Do you participate in class discussions?		

Role play

With another student, write and practice a conversation between a parent and a teacher. Talk about the child's progress in school. Present your dialogue to the class.

3 Money

How do you pay your bills, by cash, money order or check?
Do you have a checking account?
What expenses do you usually pay by check? cash? credit card? money order?

Read

Many people prefer to use checks instead of cash or money orders. They use checks to pay their rent, take care of household bills, and make purchases at department stores. Checks have advantages. Checks are cheaper than money orders. When you make a purchase, you can pay by check instead of carrying a large amount of cash with you. Your cancelled checks are your receipts for payment. You can cash your paycheck or other checks for free at the bank. Money is safer in the bank than at home. In most banks, your money is insured by the government up to $100,000.

There are many kinds of checking accounts to choose from. Some are free but you have to keep a minimum balance in your account. Others require you to pay a service charge or to pay for each check that you write. Some accounts pay you interest on the amount you keep in your account. Some banks offer additional services if you have a checking account with them, such as an ATM (Automatic Teller Machine) card.

Some businesses, such as restaurants and gas stations, will accept credit cards, but they will not accept a check for payment. When you pay by check, you usually must show some form of identification with your signature or photo on it, such as a driver's license.

Read each sentence. If it is true, write T. If it is false, write F.

_____ 1. If a bank is robbed, you can lose your money.

_____ 2. If a bank goes out of business, you can lose your money.

_____ 3. If you have an account at a bank, you have to pay a fee to cash your paycheck.

_____ 4. Some checking accounts are free.

_____ 5. All businesses accept payment by check.

Listen, Read and Say

Clerk: The TV plus tax is $531.89.
Julia: Do you take personal checks?
Clerk: If it's a local bank, yes. We only need to see your driver's license.
Julia: Who do I make the check out to?
Clerk: Top Appliances.
Julia: Here's my check and my driver's license.

Practice this model with the checks below.

> A: How much is this ___***bathrobe***___ ?
> B: It's ___**$67.15**___ including tax.
> A: Who do I make the check out to?
> B: To ___**Lane Clothing**___ .

Sofia Kimelman   452
45 Collins Avenue
Miami, Florida 33141 _____

Pay to the
order of __**Lane Clothing**__ $ **67.15**

__**Sixty-seven** ¹⁵⁄₁₀₀_____ dollars

Memo __*bathrobe*__   **Sofia Kimelman**

Sofia Kimelman   453
45 Collins Avenue
Miami, Florida 33141 _____

Pay to the
order of __**Finest Fashions**__ $ **79.95**

__**Seventy-nine** ⁹⁵⁄₁₀₀_____ dollars

Memo __*sweater*__   **Sofia Kimelman**

Sofia Kimelman   454
45 Collins Avenue
Miami, Florida 33141 _____

Pay to the
order of __**Turner's**__ $ **113.50**

__**One hundred and thirteen** ⁵⁰⁄₁₀₀_____ dollars

Memo __*jacket*__   **Sofia Kimelman**

Sofia Kimelman   455
45 Collins Avenue
Miami, Florida 33141 _____

Pay to the
order of __**Artex Electronics**__ $ **367.18**

__**Three hundred sixty seven** ¹⁸⁄₁₀₀_____ dollars

Memo __*microwave*__   **Sofia Kimelman**

Sofia Kimelman   456
45 Collins Avenue
Miami, Florida 33141 _____

Pay to the
order of __**Barney's Appliances**__ $ **580.98**

__**Five hundred eighty** ⁹⁸⁄₁₀₀_____ dollars

Memo __*stereo*__   **Sofia Kimelman**

Sofia Kimelman   457
45 Collins Avenue
Miami, Florida 33141 _____

Pay to the
order of __**Boston Furniture**__ $**1040.70**

__**One thousand and forty** ⁷⁰⁄₁₀₀_____ dollars

Memo __*living room set*__   **Sofia Kimelman**

Make out these checks for the items on the left. Print your name and address on the lines on the top left of the check. Write the date on the top right line of the check.

291

Pay to the
order of _____ $ _____

_____ dollars

Memo _____ _____

$296.18
Clothes for Him

292

Pay to the
order of _____ $ _____

_____ dollars

Memo _____ _____

$876.30
Top Mart

293

Pay to the
order of _____ $ _____

_____ dollars

Memo _____ _____

$1,153.14
Jay's Jewelry

Read and discuss this bank statement for a checking account. Then, in the list below, complete the sentences about the bank statement or circle the correct word or words that make the sentence correct.

BANK STATEMENT

Central City Bank

Terry Roberts
372 Stone Street
Tucson, Arizona 85201

Statement Date: 5/15
Account Number: 113755

Account Summary

Previous Date	Previous Balance	Deposits	Interest Paid	Total Checks	Service Charge	Ending Balance
4/15	$985.14	$780.00	$3.19	$771.29		$997.04

ALL TRANSACTIONS BY DATE:

DATE	DESCRIPTION	AMOUNT	BALANCE
4/15			985.14
4/16	CHECK NUMBER 233	65.00	920.14
4/16	CHECK NUMBER 237	37.80	882.34
4/25	DEPOSIT	390.00	1272.34
4/25	CHECK NUMBER 235	500.19	772.15
4/25	CHECK NUMBER 234	42.00	730.15
5/1	DEPOSIT	390.00	1120.15
5/1	CHECK NUMBER 238	126.30	993.85
5/14	INTEREST PAID	3.19	997.04

1. The previous balance was $_____.

2. Terry deposited $_____ in her account this statement.

3. The bank paid $_____ in interest.

4. The total of all her checks was $_____.

5. She _***paid / didn't pay***_ a service charge.

6. Her ending balance was $_____.

7. Check number 234 was for $_____.

8. On 5/1 Terry deposited $_____.

9. Check number 235 cleared on _____.

10. Check number 236 _***cleared / didn't clear***_ on this statement.

Interaction

Ask another student about paying bills. Fill in the information about your partner on the chart below.

How do you pay _____?   I pay _____.

	cash	by check	by money order	with a credit card
your rent / mortgage				
your telephone bill				
your utilities				
at the supermarket				
for airline tickets				
your car insurance				
your doctor bills				
for clothes				

Putting It Together

The following chart describes the basic features of five bank accounts. Discuss the chart and answer the questions about the accounts.

ACCOUNTS

Account	Checks	Service Charge	Minimum Balance*	Interest
Basic Checking	$.30 each	none	none	none
Regular Checking	unlimited	$7.00 per month	none	none
Checking Plus	unlimited	none	1000	4.0%
Regular Savings	none	none	100	4.5%
Money Market Savings	three per month	none	500	5.0
[Money Orders		$1.00 each]		

*There is a $7.00 service charge for all accounts which fall below the minimum balance.

1. Which account has free checking?
2. Which accounts have unlimited checks?
3. Which acounts require no minimum balance?
4. Which account has the highest interest rate?
5. Which account has a per-check fee?
6. What will happen if an account falls below the minimum balance?

Putting
It
Together

These people have decided to open bank accounts. Discuss which account(s) on the previous page is (are) the best for Mr. and Mrs. DeCarlo. Which is the best for Victor? Write your reasons below.

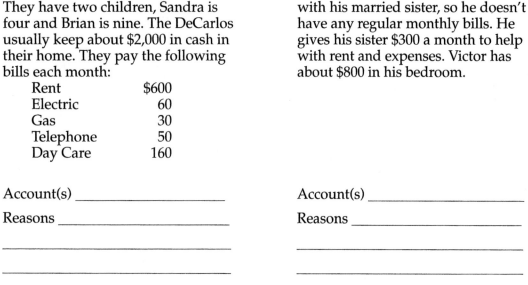

Mr. and Mrs. DeCarlo both work. They have two children, Sandra is four and Brian is nine. The DeCarlos usually keep about $2,000 in cash in their home. They pay the following bills each month:

Rent	$600
Electric	60
Gas	30
Telephone	50
Day Care	160

Account(s) _____

Reasons _____

_____

_____

Victor works full time and lives with his married sister, so he doesn't have any regular monthly bills. He gives his sister $300 a month to help with rent and expenses. Victor has about $800 in his bedroom.

Account(s) _____

Reasons _____

_____

_____

Which account(s) on the previous page would be the best for you? Why?

_____

_____

_____

Go to a local bank. Ask for information on their checking and savings accounts. Report the information to your class. Compare the accounts offered at different banks in your area.

FIND OUT

4 Shopping

Discuss

What appliances do you have in your home?"
Which of your appliances are still under warranty or guarantee?
Did you ever have a problem with an appliance you bought?
If so, what did you do about it?

Read

When buying electronic equipment or a major appliance, it is difficult to choose among the many name brands and special features. To help you decide which model to buy, there are several consumer magazines which rate these items. Local libraries have copies of these magazines in their reference sections.

Once you decide on a model, you should compare the prices at several stores. Talk to the salesperson and ask questions about several models. Most salespersons can explain different models and features, but don't depend on them for recommendations for the best brand or model. It is often possible to negotiate with the salesperson and get the product for less than the marked price. After you make your choice, many stores will encourage you to buy a store service contract. You rarely need a store service contract because the manufacturer provides a warranty. Appliances and electronic equipment usually don't need repair for several years.

If your appliance doesn't work within the warranty period, you should return the item as soon as possible and the store will repair it or replace it with a new one. If the appliance is a large item, such as a refrigerator, the company will send their own repairperson. Sometimes you have to send smaller items directly to the manufacturer.

Read each sentence. If it is true, write T. If it is false, write F.

_____ 1. A salesperson always knows the best model to buy.

_____ 2. You can usually bargain for a better price in electronics and appliance stores.

_____ 3. It is necessary to get a store service contract when you buy a new CD player.

_____ 4. If your TV breaks soon after you buy it, the store or manufacturer will usually fix it free.

_____ 5. The seller or manufacturer will always give you a new appliance if yours breaks.

Mrs. Garcia: I bought this coffee maker here last month, but it doesn't work right.
Salesperson: What's the problem?
Mrs. Garcia: The coffee doesn't stay hot.
Salesperson: We'll send it back to the manufacturer and give you a new one.
Mrs. Garcia: Fine. Thank you.

Practice
Practice

Practice this model with the appliance problems below.

A: I bought this ____**toaster**____ here last week, but it doesn't work right.

B: What's the problem?

A: _____**The toast doesn't pop up.**_____

1. The toast / not pop up

2. It / not get hot
   It / not turn on / off

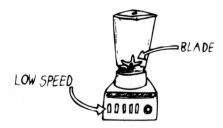

3. The low speed / not work
   The blade / not turn

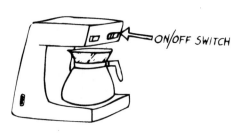

4. The coffee / not stay hot
   It / not shut off automatically

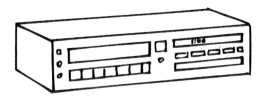

5. The tape / not rewind
   The tape / not fast-forward

6. The remote / not work
   The disk / skip

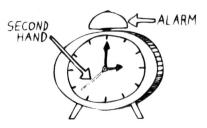

7. It / not get hot enough
   The temperature control / not work
   It / not steam

8. It / not keep the correct time
   The alarm / not ring

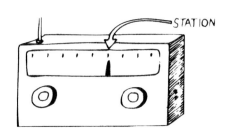

9. It / not pick up dirt from the carpet
   The switch / not work

10. It / not get good reception
    It / not hold the station

11. The timer / not work
    The defrost / not work

12. The remote / not change the channel

Partner Exercise

Explain the problem with each appliance.

Student 1

hair dryer / get hot
The hair dryer doesn't get hot.

1. hair dryer / get hot
2. switch / work
3. vacuum / pick up dirt
4. radio / get good reception

5. clock / keep the correct time

6. blade / turn
7. VCR / rewind
8. stereo / sound good
9. remote / change the channel

10. microwave / defrost

(FOLD HERE)

Student 2
Listen carefully and help Student 1.

1. The hair dryer doesn't get hot.
2. The switch doesn't work.
3. The vacuum doesn't pick up dirt.
4. The radio doesn't get good reception.
5. The clock doesn't keep the correct time.
6. The blade doesn't turn.
7. The VCR doesn't rewind.
8. The stereo doesn't sound good.
9. The remote doesn't change the channel.
10. The microwave doesn't defrost.

Complete these conversations between a customer and a clerk in an appliance store.

Clerk: Can I help you?

Juan: I'd like to return this _____. I bought it here last week, but _____.

Clerk: Do you have the receipt?

Juan: Yes. Here it is.

Clerk: Would you like to return it or get a refund?

Juan: _____.

Clerk: Henry's Appliances.

Sofia: This is Sofia Frumin. You delivered a Marvel refrigerator to us yesterday. It's not working right. It _____.

Clerk: You need to call the manufacturer. They'll send someone to look at it. Marvel's number is 284-9732.

Sofia: Thank you.

David is buying a new VCR for his home. He's at the electronics store, trying to decide which VCR to buy.

Discuss these questions.

1. What kind of store is David in?
2. What is he looking for?
3. What are some features to look for in a good VCR?
4. Do other stores have the same VCR models?
5. Does the salesperson always tell the customer what the best product is for the best price?
6. Can David bargain the price down?
7. Are the prices the same in different stores?
8. What are some problems a customer could have after he buys a VCR?
9. Can David exchange the VCR if he doesn't like the picture when he hooks it up to his TV?
10. Do most electronics stores repair the products they sell?

Sit in a small group. The following sentences give David several suggestions about buying a VCR. After you read each one and discuss it, check "agree" or "disagree."

	Agree	Disagree
1. He should look in a consumer's magazine for the quality and repair records of different models.	_____	_____
2. He should buy the VCR that the clerk recommends.	_____	_____
3. He should buy a VCR with a lot of special features.	_____	_____
4. He should choose a VCR with stereo hi-fi sound.	_____	_____
5. He should buy a VCR that is simple to program.	_____	_____
6. He should buy the least-expensive VCR.	_____	_____
7. He should compare the prices for the same model in different stores.	_____	_____
8. He should bargain down the price marked on the VCR.	_____	_____
9. He should get a service contract.	_____	_____
10. He should buy the VCR with the store's lay-away plan.	_____	_____

Your group is buying a VCR or an appliance. Write five questions you might ask the salesperson. Share your questions with other groups.

1. _____

2. _____

3. _____

4. _____

5. _____

Role play

With another student, write and practice a conversation between a salesperson and a customer in an electronics or appliance store. Ask for information about different models. Choose a model and try to negotiate a lower price.

25

5 Transportation

Did you ever ask for or give directions? Where to?
Did you ever get lost? Where were you going?
Who did you ask for directions?

Discuss

Read

When you are driving through a town or city, it is important to understand and obey traffic signs.

You must not park in this area between 11 PM and 7 AM.

You must not turn right until the traffic light is green.

You must not turn around on this street.

You must slow down because young children are probably in this area.

You must not park or wait in this area.

You must take a different route because this street is closed.

You must slow down at the intersection. The other cars have the right of way.

You must not drive into this street; traffic goes in the opposite direction.

You must stop your car. Look both ways, then continue when no traffic is coming.

You must not drive faster than thirty miles per hour in this area.

All traffic on this street must follow the direction of the arrow.

You must slow down because there are curves ahead.

Miguel:	Do you know where the courthouse is?
Officer:	Sure. Go up this street. Make a right at the first light.
	That's Mesa Avenue. The courthouse is three blocks down on the left.
Miguel:	Okay. I turn right at the first light.
Officer:	That's it. And the courthouse is down the street.
Miguel:	Thank you.

Practice this model with the following locations.

A: Do you know where ___*the hospital*___ is? *or*

Can you tell me where ___*the hospital*___ is?

B: It's ___*three*___ blocks up/down on the right/left.

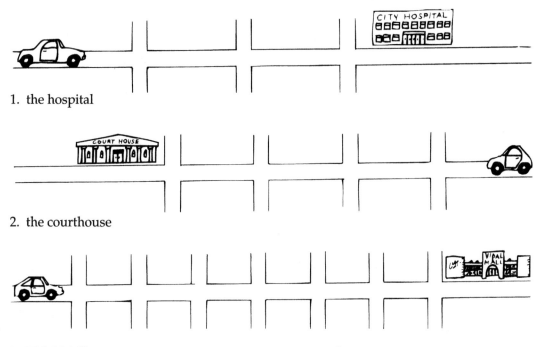

1. the hospital

2. the courthouse

3. Vidal Mall

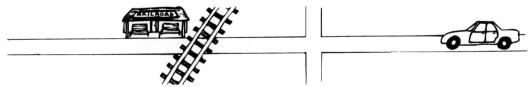

4. the train station

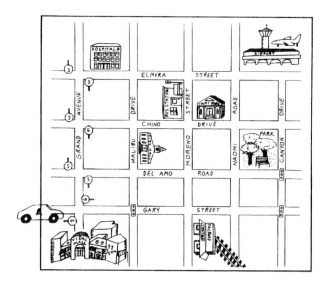

 = stop sign

= light

Sit in a small group. You're in the car on the map above. Follow these directions. Write your destination.

1. Go down Gary Street two blocks. Make a right at Moreno Street. The
   _____**train station**_____ is on the left.

2. Go down Gary Street. Make a left at the first traffic light. That's Malibu Drive.
   _____ is two blocks up on the right.

3. Turn left at this stop sign. That's Grand Avenue. Go up Grand and make a
   right at the third stop sign. You'll see the _____ on your left.

4. Go up Gary Street about five blocks. Make a left at the second traffic light. Go
   up Canyon Drive about three blocks to the _____.

5. Make a left at the corner. That's Grand Avenue. Go up two blocks. Make a
   right at Chino Drive. The _____ is three blocks down on the left.

Partner Exercise

Give the directions.

Student 1	**Student 2**
Make a ↴ 🚦🚦	*Listen carefully and help Student 1.*
Make a right at the second light.	

Student 1
Make a ↴ 🚦🚦
Make a right at the second light.

1. Make a ↴ 🚦🚦
2. Turn ↴ Chino Drive
3. Make a ↗ Ⓢ
4. Turn ↗ 🚦🚦🚦
5. Make a ↗ El Toro Road
6. Make a ↗ 🚦
7. Turn ↗ Walker Street
8. Make a ↰ Ⓢ Ⓢ

9. Turn ↴ 🚦
10. Make a ↗ Ley Road

(FOLD HERE)

Student 2
Listen carefully and help Student 1.

1. Make a right at the second light.
2. Turn right at Chino Drive.
3. Make a left at the first stop sign.
4. Turn left at the fourth light.
5. Make a left at El Toro Road.
6. Make a left at the first light.
7. Turn left at Walker Street.
8. Make a right at the second stop sign.
9. Turn right at the first light.
10. Make a left at Ley Road.

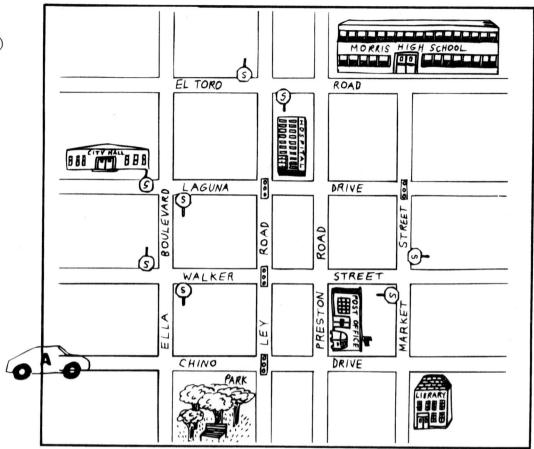

Practice this model. Give directions to the driver in the car above. He is looking for the following locations:

1. the library
2. City Hall
3. the post office
4. the hospital
5. Morris High School

Go	up down	this street	about _____ blocks. to the _____.
Make a Turn	left right	at the _____ sign. at the _____ light. at _____ Street.	

| The _____ is _____ blocks | up
down | on the | right.
left. |

Sarah is on the interstate highway, about forty miles from home. A red warning light just went on and the engine is smoking. Sarah pulled the car over onto the shoulder and turned off the car. She isn't sure what to do. The exits are about ten miles apart. She passed a service area about a mile back.

Discuss these questions.

1. Where is Sarah? Is this a busy road?
2. What time is it?
3. What's the problem?
4. How does Sarah feel? Why?
5. Is she standing in a safe place?
6. Do you think Sarah knows how to fix the engine?
7. Is this a dangerous situation? Why or why not?
8. Do you think people will stop to offer to help her?
9. How long do you think she will have to wait for the police?
10. Who will sometimes call the police or a tow truck?

Sit in a small group. The following sentences give several suggestions about Sarah's situation. After you read each one and discuss it, write "should" or "shouldn't" in the blank.

1. Sarah _____ stand in front of the car.

2. Sarah _____ stand on the grassy area next to the car.

3. Sarah _____ sit in her car and wait for help.

4. Sarah _____ stand in back of the car, directing traffic away.

5. Sarah _____ tie a white handkerchief to her door handle or antenna.

6. If she has them, Sarah _____ set out flashing lights or a reflector.

7. Sarah _____ wait for the police.

8. Sarah _____ walk back to the last service area.

9. Sarah _____ disregard the red light and drive her car to the next exit.

10. Sarah _____ ask the first person who stops to call the police at the next exit or service area.

11. Sarah _____ allow someone who stops to help her fix the car.

12. Sarah _____ accept a ride from someone who stops.

With your group, decide what Sarah should do. Write your opinion below. Share your opinion with the other groups.

_____

_____

_____

_____

1. Sit in small groups. Write directions and draw a simple map from your school to a location in your town, such as to the hospital or to the park. One person in each group will dictate the directions to the class. Does everyone agree that these are the best directions to that location?   *or*

2. Write about an experience you had getting lost or breaking down. What happened? Where were you? Who helped you? What did you do?

6 Housing

Discuss

Why did you choose your present apartment and neighborhood?

What do you like about it? What don't you like about it?

How are the schools in your neighborhood?

Read

There are many things to consider when you are looking for a place to live. Each family has to decide which things are most important to their lives. If you have a large family, the size of the apartment is important. Families with children should find out about the quality of the school system. If you don't have a car, you might prefer to find an apartment or house close to work, public transportation, or shopping. Families may prefer to live near friends or people who speak the same language.

After you decide what size apartment you need and how much rent you can afford, decide which locations in your area best meet your needs. Spend time in each area. Walk around the neighborhood. Check the schools. Drive around the area in the daytime and in the evening to see if the area is safe. When you decide on one or two neighborhoods, ask friends, look through the newspaper, and contact real estate agents to help you find an apartment or home you like.

Look at several different apartments and neighborhoods before you decide where to live. Sometimes, you may find two similar apartments for the same rent. One neighborhood may have better schools; the other may be more convenient to work. You usually can't find all of the characteristics you want in one apartment, but you will need to choose the one place that has most of the things that are important to you.

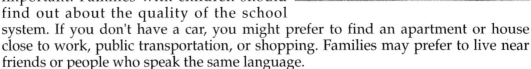

Read each sentence. If it is true, write T. If it is false, write F.

_____ 1. Every town and city has a good school system.

_____ 2. An area that is quiet in the day may be noisy and dangerous at night.

_____ 3. A real estate agent can show you several apartments in different neighborhoods.

_____ 4. The apartment with the cheapest rent is usually the best choice.

_____ 5. Apartments the same size are usually about the same rent.

Boris: Did you find a new apartment yet?

Marc: Yesterday we saw an apartment in Newport. It has two bedrooms and the rent is reasonable.

Boris: Do you think you'll take it?

Marc: We're not sure. It's smaller than our apartment now. But Newport is safer and the schools are better.

Boris: Keep looking. Maybe you'll find exactly what you want.

Read each group of words or sentences. For each number circle the sentence that best describes your apartment or neighborhood.

1. a. It's near work.	**b.** It's not too far from work.	**c.** It's far from work.
2. a. It's near public transportation.	**b.** It's not too far from transportation.	**c.** It's far from transportation.
3. a. It's in a safe neighborhood.	**b.** The neighborhood is safe most of the time.	**c.** It's in a bad neighborhood.
4. a. It's in a quiet neighborhood.	**b.** The neighborhood is quiet most of the time.	**c.** It's in a noisy neighborhood.
5. a. It's a large apartment.	**b.** It's an average size apartment.	**c.** It's a small apartment.
6. a. The rent is low.	**b.** The rent is reasonable.	**c.** The rent is high.
7. a. The schools are good.	**b.** The schools aren't too good.	**c.** The schools are bad.
8. a. My street is quiet.	**b.** There is some traffic on my street.	**c.** My street has a lot of traffic.
9. a. The neighbors are friendly.	**b.** The neighbors keep to themselves.	**c.** The neighbors are unfriendly.
10. a. There are many stores near my apt.	**b.** My apartment is not too far from stores.	**c.** My apartment is far from stores.

COMPARATIVE ADJECTIVES

small – smaller	convenient – more convenient	good – better
old – older	modern – more modern	bad – worse
busy – busier	expensive – more expensive	far – farther

Practice this model with the pictures below. Use the adjectives in the boxes to compare the apartments and the neighborhoods.

The apartment on Glen Street is __*larger*__ than the apartment on Bay Avenue.

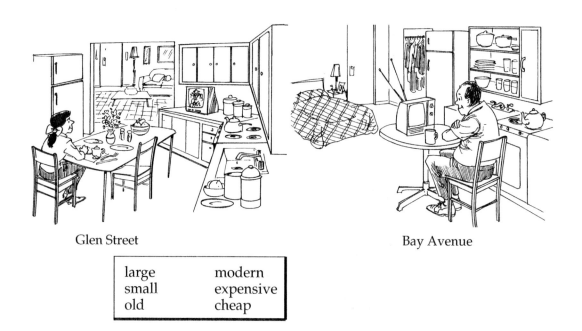

Glen Street   Bay Avenue

large	modern
small	expensive
old	cheap

Glen Street is __*quieter*__ than Bay Avenue.

Glen Street   Bay Avenue

quiet	dirty	attractive
noisy	safe	nice
clean	dangerous	pretty

Partner Exercise

Talk about these apartments for rent.

Student 1	**Student 2**
neighborhood / safe	*Listen carefully and help Student 1.*
The neighborhood is safer.	

1. neighborhood / safe	1. The neighborhood is safer.
2. neighborhood / attractive	2. The neighborhood is more attractive.
3. neighborhood / convenient	3. The neighborhood is more convenient.
4. neighborhood / noisy	4. The neighborhood is noisier.
5. neighborhood / dangerous	5. The neighborhood is more dangerous.
6. neighbors / friendly	6. The neighbors are friendlier.
7. apartment / far from work	7. The apartment is farther from work.
8. apartment / close to work	8. The apartment is closer to work.
9. apartment / good	9. The apartment is better.
10. rent / expensive	10. The rent is more expensive.

(FOLD HERE)

Complete these sentences. Compare your apartment to the apartment on Main Street. Use the comparative of one of the adjectives in parentheses.

1. The apartment on Main Street is $625 a month. My rent is _____.
   (cheap / expensive / the same)

2. There are about two crimes a month on Main Street. My neighborhood is
   _____. (safe / dangerous / the same)

3. The apartment on Main Street has two bedrooms. My apartment is
   _____. (small / large / the same size)

4. The apartment on Main Street is ten miles from work. My apartment is
   _____. (close / far / the same distance)

5. The elementary school near Main Street is okay. The elementary school near
   my apartment is _____. (good / bad / the same)

6. People throw cans and bottles on Main Street. My neighborhood is
   _____. (clean / dirty / the same)

7. The apartment on Main Street is eighty years old. My apartment is
   _____. (old / new / the same age)

8. Main Street is busy at rush hour. My street is _____. (quiet / busy /
   the same)

9. There is a bus stop one block from the apartment on Main Street. My
   apartment is _____ public transportation. (close to / far from)

10. I think my apartment is _____ (good / bad) than the apartment on
    Main Street.

Nelson and Sonia live in a two-bedroom apartment in Verona with their two boys, who are nine and twelve. Nelson's mother is coming to live with them and she needs a separate bedroom. These are the two apartments Nelson and Sonia liked the best. Each has advantages and disadvantages. Talk about the layout of each apartment, then discuss the questions below.

Bedroom	Bedroom	Bathroom	Bedroom
Bathroom	Living Room		Kitchen

Bedroom	Bathroom	Bedroom	Kitchen
Bedroom	Living Room		Dining Room

rent—$650 a month
stores and transportation—one mile
park—one mile away
very good schools
a safe neighborhood
quiet area, little traffic
people keep to themselves
no families in the neighborhood
   speak their language

rent—$600 a month
stores and transportation—two blocks
park—one block away
good schools
usually a safe neighborhood
noisy area, busy streets
people are friendly
some families in the neighborhood
   speak their language

1. Which apartment is larger?
2. Which apartment has a better layout? Why?
3. Which apartment is more expensive?
4. Which apartment is more convenient?
5. In which neighborhood are the neighbors friendlier?

Sit in a small group and discuss these questions. Write your opinion and reasons. Share your ideas with the other groups.

1. Which neighborhood is better for Nelson's mother? Why?

_____

_____

2. Which neighborhood is better for the children? Why?

_____

_____

3. Which apartment should they rent? Why?

_____

_____

Ask another student these questions about his or her house or apartment. Fill in the chart below with information about your partner's apartment and your apartment.

QUESTIONS	YOUR PARTNER	YOU
Where do you live?		
Do you live in a house or in an apartment?		
Is your apartment big enough for you?		
Is the rent reasonable?		
How are the schools?		
Is your neighborhood safe? Why or why not?		
Is your neighborhood noisy? If so, why?		
How far are you from public transportation?		
How far are you from work?		
Is your apartment convenient to stores?		
Do any people in your neighborhood speak your language?		
Do you like your apartment? Why or why not?		

Write a composition about your apartment or house and neighborhood. What do you like about your apartment and neighborhood? What don't you like about your apartment and neighborhood? Give several examples.

7 Community Resources

Discuss

What activities do you enjoy doing in your free time?
What are your hobbies?
What activities or sports do your children participate in after school or outside of school?

Read

Schools, colleges, and organizations in most communities offer residents an opportunity to study in evening and Saturday classes. Those who are interested in job skills can study business and clerical courses, or they can get technical instruction in subjects such as computers, auto mechanics, or carpentry. Leisure time courses, such as crafts, music, dance, photography, and sports, are also offered. Many of the community courses are hands on and you can participate with beginning or intermediate English skills.

Most American children participate in after-school and weekend activities. These activities are supervised by schools, religious organizations, and private studios, or by community groups, such as the Girl Scouts and Boy Scouts. Some programs emphasize dance, gymnastics, music, camping, and sports programs. In other programs, children plan and participate in community activities to develop a better understanding of their values and the people around them.

To find more information, you can stop at or call City Hall, the Y, the Board of Education, colleges, private studios, museums, the library, and other organizations in your area. These groups have brochures or lists of their courses, times, and fees. Many courses, especially those sponsored by local organizations, are free or low cost. Private dance, art, or music lessons can be expensive.

Read each sentence. If it is true, write T. If it is false, write F.

_____ 1. Adults can take courses to improve their job skills.

_____ 2. A person needs to speak English well to take an art class.

_____ 3. After-school activities are only for fun.

_____ 4. Most after-school programs are expensive.

_____ 5. American parents want their children to participate in after-school programs.

Secretary: Good afternoon.

Diego: Good afternoon. I'm interested in taking a word-processing course.

Secretary: We have two courses, beginning and intermediate.

Diego: I need the beginning course. When does it meet?

Secretary: It meets on Thursdays, from 6:40 to 9:30.

Diego: That's a good time for me. How much does it cost?

Secretary: It costs $125.

Diego: When does the course begin?

Secretary: It begins next Thursday and it runs for ten weeks.

Diego: Good. How can I register?

Secretary: Fill out this registration form and return it with the $125 fee as soon as possible. The course is almost filled.

Diego: I'll bring it in tomorrow. Thank you.

Practice this model with the courses below.

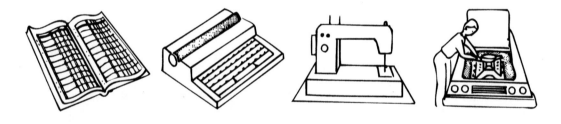

I'm interested in taking a/an ___*accounting*___ course.

1. accounting   2. typing   3. sewing   4. auto mechanics

5. GED (high school equivalency)   6. photography   7. computer programming   8. English

Practice this model with the adult education courses below.

A: When does the _____ course meet?

B: It meets on _____ from _____ to _____.

A: How much does it cost?

B: It costs $ _____.

A: When does the course begin?

B: It begins _____.

A: And how long does it run?

B: It runs for _____ weeks.

CS 34 WORD PROCESSING 1   Room 154 $80
MONDAY 7:00–9:00   SEPT. 10   10 weeks   Trudy Kling
This course is designed to teach the basics of word processing, using an
IBM compatible personal computer.

PI 25 FREEDOM FROM SMOKING   Room 130 $25
WEDNESDAY   8:00–9:30   SEPT. 19   4 weeks   Dan Higgins
Has it been difficult for you to stop smoking? Certified clinic leader will
help smokers understand their habit and quit smoking.

SR 81 YOGA   Room 17 $52
TUESDAY   7:00–8:30   SEPT. 25   8 weeks   Barbara Gold
Relax; forget stress and tension. Learn traditional Yoga postures, breathing,
and how to use your body in a healthy way.

CA ACRYLIC PAINTING   Studio 3 $72
THURSDAY   7:00–9:00   SEPT. 18   10 weeks   Bruce Long
Learn about form, light, and color with water soluble acrylic paints.
Develop compositions working from sketches and still life.

MT 45 GUITAR FOR BEGINNERS   Room 115 $48
MONDAY   8:00–9:30   SEPT. 12   8 weeks   Mel Blackman
You'll learn basic chord fingering, simple melodies, and popular tunes. Book
is an additional $6 at first class.

AE 71 INTRODUCTION TO TRAVEL AND TOURISM Room 233 $90
MONDAY and WEDNESDAY   7:00–8:30   6 weeks   Joan Dunkel
An introduction to the day-to-day operation of a travel agency, including
ticketing, hotels, tours, and accounting systems.

Partner Exercise

Ask and answer questions about these adult education courses.

<table>
<tr><td>

Student 1
When / photography course / meet?
When does the photography course meet?

1. When / art / meet?
2. Thursdays / 8:15–9:30

3. How much / cost?
4. $40 plus supplies
5. When / begin?
6. January 25
7. When / typing course / meet?
8. Mondays and Wednesdays / 7:30–9:30
9. How much / cost?
10. $90
11. How long / run?
12. ten weeks

</td><td>

(FOLD HERE)

</td><td>

Student 2
Listen carefully and help Student 1.

1. When does the art course meet?
2. It meets on Thursdays from 8:15 to 9:30.
3. How much does it cost?
4. It costs $40 plus supplies.
5. When does it begin?
6. It begins on January 25.
7. When does the typing course meet?
8. It meets on Mondays and Wednesdays from 7:30 to 9:30.
9. How much does it cost?
10. It costs $90.
11. How long does it run?
12. It runs for ten weeks.

</td></tr>
</table>

Complete the questions for the courses below.

LR 32 AUTO MECHANICS 1   Room 131 $35
MONDAY   7:30–9:30   SEPT. 14   5 weeks   Charles Glatt
General auto maintenance and repairs. Learn to give your car a tune-up.
Classes are hands-on.

---

1. When ___*does the course meet*___ ?   Mondays from 7:30 to 9:30.

2. When _____ ?   On September 14.

3. How much _____ ? $35.

4. How long _____ ?   For five weeks.

CL 20 PHOTOGRAPHY (BEGINNING)   Room 212 $40
TUESDAY   8:00–9:30   OCT. 2   6 weeks   William Aftra
Introduction to use and handling of 35mm camera. Learn about picture
composition, types of film, and darkroom processing.

---

5. When _____ ?   Tuesdays from 8:00 to 9:30.

6. When _____ ?   On October 2.

7. How much _____ ? $40.

8. How long _____ ?   For six weeks.

Interaction

Ask another student about his or her interests. Fill in the chart below with information about your partner and about yourself.

Are you interested in taking a course in _____?

	YOUR PARTNER		YOU	
	Yes	No	Yes	No
1. aerobics				
2. swimming				
3. self-defense				
4. karate				
5. photography				
6. word processing				
7. art				
8. drama				
9. dance				
10. starting your own business				
11. real estate				
12. financial investing				
13. cooking				

1. What are you interested in taking? Why?

   _____

   _____

2. What is your experience in this activity?

   _____

   _____

   _____

Find Out *Stop at the local Y, adult school, or another program in your area. Ask for information about the different kinds of courses and services offered by the program. Find out about the location, hours, and costs. Report the information to your class.*

Kim Park is in the fifth grade. Her school offers several after-school activities, but she doesn't participate in any. Many girls in her class belong to the Girl Scouts. They meet in the school cafeteria twice a month on Mondays after school. A few volunteer mothers lead the activities. Kim wants to join, but Mrs. Park is nervous about Kim joining an organization. She never belonged to any clubs when she was a girl. Also, Mrs. Park works full time and is more secure knowing that Kim is home right after school every day. Today the Girl Scout troop is learning about fire safety. Next week, they will visit the local fire station.

Discuss these questions.

1. What organization do these children belong to?
2. When and where do they meet?
3. What are the girls doing in each picture? Who is supervising them?
4. Why are these kinds of activities important?
5. Do the parents have to volunteer to help in order for their girls to belong to this organization?
6. Should Mrs. Park let her daughter join the Girl Scouts?
7. What are some groups that offer after-school activities in your town?

8 Doctors

Discuss

Do you have a regular doctor or do you go to a clinic?
Is it difficult to get an appointment?
What kind of doctors do you see?
How can you find the name of a good doctor?

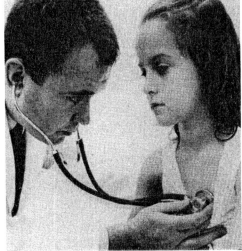

Read

Medical care in the United States is very specialized. Typically, families go to private doctors or to clinics for their medical care. Family doctors who take care of everyday medical problems are called general practitioners, internists, or pediatricians for children. When patients have a specific problem that is serious or continues for a long time, they go to a specialist. People will also consult specialists, such as cardiologists (heart) or gastroenterologists (stomach), for a second opinion.

Sometimes, your family doctor will refer you to a specialist. Other times you might go directly, without a referral. At hospital clinics, patients first see a general practitioner; then the doctor refers the patient to a specialist within the clinic or at another hospital.

In many urban areas, there are hospitals that specialize in specific problems. The hospitals might specialize in orthopedics, cardiology, cancer, or other areas. These hospitals often have clinics with medical fees based on income.

Read each sentence. If it is true, write T. If it is false, write F.

_____ 1. Patients only see specialists for life-and-death medical problems.

_____ 2. A patient might see a cardiologist for frequent chest pains.

_____ 3. It is possible to see a specialist without a referral.

_____ 4. If a doctor recommends surgery, a patient should go to another specialist for a second opinion.

_____ 5. If you cannot afford to see a specialist, some clinics provide medical care based on your salary.

Charles: This is Charles Pierre. I'd like to make an appointment for my daughter with Doctor Bronton.

Nurse: What's the problem?

Charles: Her chest is bothering her. It hurts when she coughs.

Nurse: Can you bring her in on Thursday at 2:00?

Charles: I can't make it then. I'm working. Can I come in later on Thursday?

Nurse: How about 4:45?

Charles: That's good. Thank you.

Nurse: We'll see you at 4:45.

Practice this model with the health problems below.

Her chest ____ is bothering ____ **her.** It hurts when **she coughs.** ____	**His eyes** ____ are bothering ____ **him.** They hurt when **he reads.** ____

1. Her chest
   cough

2. His eyes
   read

3. Her throat
   swallow

4. My neck
   turn my head

5. His knees
   play any sport

6. My back
   bend over

7. His shoulder
   raise his arm

8. My arm
   move it

9. Her jaw
   chew

45

Partner Exercise

Describe these medical problems.

Student 1

My son's chest / cough
My son's chest is bothering him.
It hurts when he coughs.

1. My son's chest
   cough
2. His throat
   swallow
3. My legs
   stand a long time
4. Her eyes
   use a computer
5. Her back
   pick up the baby
6. My jaw
   chew
7. My daughter's feet
   run
8. His neck
   drive
9. My son's shoulder
   play baseball
10. My eyes
    watch TV

(FOLD HERE)

Student 2
Listen carefully and help Student 1.

1. My son's chest is bothering him.
   It hurts when he coughs.
2. His throat is bothering him.
   It hurts when he swallows.
3. My legs are bothering me.
   They hurt when I stand a long time.
4. Her eyes are bothering her.
   They hurt when she uses a computer.
5. Her back is bothering her.
   It hurts when she picks up the baby.
6. My jaw is bothering me.
   It hurts when I chew.
7. My daughter's feet are bothering her.
   They hurt when she runs.
8. His neck is bothering him.
   It hurts when he drives.
9. My son's shoulder is bothering him.
   It hurts when he plays baseball.
10. My eyes are bothering me.
    They hurt when I watch TV.

Interaction

Ask two students these questions about their doctors. Fill in their answers on the chart below.

	STUDENT 1	STUDENT 2
Do you go to a family doctor or to a clinic?		
What is the doctor or clinic's name?		
How much is an office visit?		
Is it easy to get an appointment?		
Why do you like this doctor or clinic?		

Practice this model to arrange a doctor's appointment with the times and reasons below. Use your own name and give a health problem.

A: This is _____ .

  I'd like to make an appointment with the doctor.

  My _____ is bothering me. _____ .

B: Can you come in ___tomorrow___ at ___2:00___ ?

A: I can't make it then. ___I'm working___ .

B: How about ___tomorrow___ at ___5:00___ ?

A: That's fine.

1. tomorrow   2:00
   I'm working.
   tomorrow   5:00

2. Friday   9:00
   I'm at school.
   Friday   3:00

3. today   10:00
   I have another appointment
   today   2:00

Complete these conversations between a nurse and a patient.

1. Patient: _____ an appointment with Doctor Thomas.

   Nurse: What's the problem?

   Patient: My _____ bothering me. _____ when

              _____ .

   Nurse: Can you come in _____ at _____ ?

   Patient: I can't make it then. I _____ .

   Nurse: How about _____ ?

   Patient: That's fine.

2. Patient: _____ an appointment with Doctor Larson.

   Nurse: What's the problem?

   Patient: _____ bothering _____ . _____

              when _____ .

   Nurse: Can you come in _____ at _____ ?

   Patient: I can't make it then. I _____ .

   Nurse: How about _____ at _____ ?

   Patient: That's good.

Bob and Emily have two sons, Adam is twelve and Steven is seven. Steven woke up this morning with a low fever, a runny nose, and a sore throat. Emily has to leave for work in thirty minutes. Her husband already left for work. Talk about what is happening in the picture.

Sit in a small group. The following sentences give Emily advice. After you read each one and discuss it, write "should" or "shouldn't" in the blank.

1. Emily _____ take off from work and stay home with Steven.

2. Emily _____ leave Steven home alone.

3. Emily _____ leave Steven home alone and ask a neighbor to check on him from time to time.

4. Emily _____ try to find a babysitter.

5. Emily _____ tell Adam, who is twelve, to stay home with his little brother.

6. Emily _____ give Steven some cold medicine and send him to school.

7. Emily _____ send Steven to school but tell him to go to the nurse if he feels worse.

8. Emily _____ take Steven to the doctor today.

9. Emily _____ wait until tomorrow to see if Steven really needs to go to the doctor.

10. The doctor is off today. Emily _____ take Steven to the emergency room.

With your group, decide what Emily should do. Write your opinion below. Share your opinion with other groups.

_____

_____

These are twelve medical specialists. Pronounce the names after the teacher. Talk about each speciality. What kinds of problems does each specialist treat?

a. allergist

b. cardiologist

c. dermatologist

d. urologist

e. physical therapist

f. orthopedist

g. obstetrician / gynecologist

h. opthalmologist / optometrist

i. eye, ear, nose, and throat specialist

j. gastroenterologist

k. psychiatrist / psychologist

l. neurologist

Your family doctor or pediatrician will refer you to a specialist if a problem is persistent or serious. Write the letter of the correct specialist for each situation below.

_____ 1. My mother has some chest pains.

_____ 2. My eyes hurt when I read.

_____ 3. My child has frequent ear infections.

_____ 4. My period is two weeks late. I think I'm pregnant.

_____ 5. I often get stomach cramps and have gas.

_____ 6. In the spring and fall I sneeze a lot and my eyes water.

_____ 7. My husband broke his leg when he was playing basketball.

_____ 8. My son has terrible migraine headaches.

_____ 9. My daughter has bad acne.

_____ 10. My father is nervous and upset all the time. He's very depressed.

_____ 11. I have pain when I urinate.

_____ 12. My mother broke her leg and needs to learn how to walk with crutches.

Role play

With another student, write and practice a conversation between a nurse and a patient. Describe the problem and make an appointment. Present your dialogue to the class.

9 Emergencies

Discuss

Did you ever go to the hospital emergency room? Why did you go?
When should you go to the emergency room?
Where else can you go in an emergency?
What kind of medical insurance do you have?

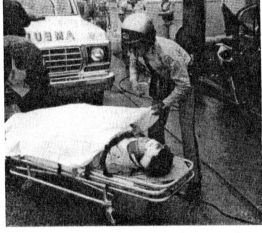

Read

You can get treatment for serious medical problems in the emergency room of a hospital. These problems include heart attack, broken bones, serious bleeding, animal bites, or serious burns. Go to the emergency room for sudden serious pain, such as chest or stomach pains. For common health problems such as colds, fevers, and rashes, you should go to your family doctor. Do not go to the emergency room for chronic problems or problems you can make a doctor's appointment for. If possible, call your own doctor before you go to the emergency room. If you want her to treat you, you must go to the hospital she is associated with.

Hospital emergency rooms are open twenty-four hours a day. They are often crowded and you might have to wait a long time to see a doctor. When the doctor examines you, she will ask many questions about your specific injury or condition. She will also ask if you have any allergies, what medications you are presently taking, and your medical history. Sometimes you might need X-rays or special laboratory tests. Usually, the emergency room releases you the same day. They will tell you to go to a doctor outside the hospital for follow-up treatment. If your condition is serious, you might have to stay in the hospital

Treatment at the hospital emergency room is more expensive than in a doctor's office. If you have medical insurance, bring your insurance ID card with you.

Read each sentence. If it is true, write T. If it is false, write F.

_____ 1. You should go to the emergency room when you have a bad cold.

_____ 2. Your doctor can treat you in the emergency room.

_____ 3. You may have to wait two or three hours to see a doctor in the emergency room.

_____ 4. You should go to the emergency room for follow-up treatment.

_____ 5. It's cheaper to go to a doctor than to the emergency room.

Nurse: What's the problem?
Rita: My son was playing on the swing when he fell off and cut his chin.
Nurse: What's his name?
Rita: Michael Ruiz.
Nurse: Do you have medical insurance?
Rita: Yes.
Nurse: Can I see your ID card?
Rita: Here.
Nurse: Thank you. Just have a seat. We'll call you.

Practice this model with the emergencies below.

A: What's the problem?
B: ___*My son fell off the swing*___ and ___*cut his chin.*___

1. My son / fall off   cut   2. My husband / fall off   break

3. My sister / touch   burn   4. My wife / faint   hit

5. My father / slip   sprain   6. My brother / lift   hurt

Practice this model with the situations below.

> A: What's the problem?
>
> B: _____**My son**_____ was _____*playing on the swing*_____
>
> when _*he fell off and cut his chin.*_

1. My son / play on swing   fall off   cut

2. My husband / paint the ceiling   fall off   break

3. My sister / cook dinner   touch   burn

4. My wife / stand in line   faint   hit

5. My brother / move furniture   lift   pull

Partner Exercise

Explain each injury.

Student 1

My sister stand in line / faint / hit her head
My sister was standing in line when she fainted and hit her head.

1. My sister stand in line / faint / hit her head
2. My daughter / climb a tree / fall / break her arm
3. My husband / walk home / slip on the ice / hit his head

4. My son / roller blade / fall / sprain his ankle
5. My son / fix his car / touch the engine / burn his hand

6. My wife / wash the dishes / break a glass / cut her hand

7. My daughter / ride her bicycle / fall off / cut her chin
8. My brother / ski / fall / break his knee
9. My wife / walk upstairs / trip on a toy / break her ankle

10. My son / play / step on a piece of glass / cut his foot

(FOLD HERE)

Student 2
Listen carefully and help Student 1.

1. My sister was standing in line when she fainted and hit her head.
2. My daughter was climbing a tree when she fell and broke her arm.
3. My husband was walking home when he slipped on the ice and hit his head.
4. My son was roller blading when he fell and sprained his ankle.
5. My son was fixing his car when he touched the engine and burned his hand.
6. My wife was washing the dishes when she broke a glass and cut her hand.
7. My daughter was riding her bicycle when she fell off and cut her chin.
8. My brother was skiing when he fell and broke his knee.
9. My wife was walking upstairs when she tripped on a toy and broke her ankle.
10. My son was playing when he stepped on a piece of glass and cut his foot.

Complete these conversations between a doctor and a patient.

1. Doctor: What happened?

   Luis: I _____ (play) basketball with my son when I _____ (fall) down and _____ (sprain) my ankle.

2. Doctor: What's the problem?

   Hoang: I _____ (ride) my bicycle when I _____ (fall) off. I think I _____ (break) my arm.

3. Doctor: What's the matter with your back?

   Jean: I'm not sure. I _____ (get) a flat tire yesterday. I _____ (take) out the spare tire when I _____ (feel) a sharp pain in my back. I think I _____ (pull) a muscle.

4. Doctor: What happened?

   Mrs. Mako: My son and his friends _____ (play) with firecrackers when one _____ (explode) in his hand and _____ (burn) his hand and his arm.

Derek Wilson was playing outside with his brother. The neighbor's dog ran into their yard and bit Derek's leg. His mother put a towel on the cut and drove him to the emergency room. The cut isn't bleeding anymore and his mother doesn't know if he needs stitches or not. There are many serious injuries in the emergency room this afternoon.

Discuss these questions.

1. What's wrong with each person in the waiting area of the emergency room?
2. Do you agree with Mrs. Wilson's decision to take Derek to the emergency room?
3. How long do you think Derek will have to wait for a doctor?
4. What do you think the doctor will do?
5. Which patients may need X-rays?
6. Which patients may need stitches?
7. Which patients may need an EKG?
8. Which patients may need to see a specialist? Which specialist?
9. Which patients may need to stay in the hospital overnight?
10. What other kinds of treatments or tests will these patients need?

Sit in a small group. After you read each statement and discuss it, check "Agree" or "Disagree."

	Agree	Disagree
1. When you call an ambulance in this town, it always arrives quickly.	_____	_____
2. You can tell the ambulance to take you to the hospital of your choice.	_____	_____
3. If you need an ambulance in this town, you must call the police.	_____	_____
4. You need to bring your insurance card or money when you go to the emergency room.	_____	_____
5. An emergency room visit is cheaper than a visit to a doctor's office.	_____	_____
6. In this city, a hospital can refuse to treat you if you don't have insurance and cannot pay.	_____	_____
7. You can call your own doctor to treat you in the emergency room.	_____	_____
8. If you have sudden sharp stomach pains, you should go to the emergency room.	_____	_____
9. If you have had a bad cold and a fever for two days, you should go to the emergency room.	_____	_____
10. If your child has a fever of 105°F, you should take him to the emergency room.	_____	_____

Interaction

Ask another student these questions about an emergency room situation. Fill in the information on the chart below.

Who needed emergency attention?	
What hospital did you go to?	
What was the injury or medical problem?	
How long did you wait in the waiting room?	
What did the doctor do?	

Write about yourself or a person in your family who had an injury or a medical problem and needed to go to the emergency room. Describe the emergency in detail. What happened in the emergency room?

10 Family Events

Discuss

What family events did you celebrate this past year?

How did you celebrate them?

Did you attend a wedding recently? Who got married?

Where was the wedding?

Read

June and August are the most popular months for weddings in the United States. The type of wedding ceremony and the reception that the couple plans are determined by their religion, culture, and economic background.

Before getting married, a couple has to get a marriage license. Most states require a blood test and have various age and waiting period restrictions. If a couple wants a small simple wedding, they can have the wedding at City Hall. A justice of the peace performs the wedding in front of two witnesses. Most Americans, however, have religious ceremonies. These are performed by a minister, rabbi, or priest. The ceremony is in a church, temple, catering hall, or house.

At a typical wedding, the bride wears a long white wedding gown. The groom wears a tuxedo. The wedding party usually consists of a maid of honor and two or three bridesmaids. The groom has a best man and two or three ushers. After the guests are seated, the father of the bride walks his daughter down the center aisle. He "gives away" his daughter to the groom. During the ceremony, the couple exchanges wedding vows and rings.

There is a reception for invited guests after the wedding. These parties can be very simple or large and expensive. The bride's family traditionally pays for the reception. Typically, the reception takes place in a church hall, a catering hall, or at home. Most receptions have a band or disc jockey and the guests dance, talk, and eat. Guests at the reception give money or a present to the bride and groom.

Read each sentence. If it is true, write T. If it is false, write F.

_____ 1. Most American weddings are similar.

_____ 2. Most Americans get married at City Hall.

_____ 3. The people who attend the wedding ceremony are always invited to the reception.

_____ 4. The groom's family usually pays for the wedding reception.

_____ 5. It is acceptable to give money for a gift at a wedding.

Tuan: How was your cousin's wedding?

Kim: Beautiful! They had the reception outside under a big tent. It was sunny and warm, a perfect day.

Tuan: Did they have a lot of people?

Kim: Yes, there were about 125 people. We have a big famly and it was nice seeing them all.

Tuan: How was the food?

Kim: Really good! They had a large buffet with both Vietnamese and American food.

Tuan: Was there a disc jockey or a band?

Kim: A band. My cousin's brother is a drummer in a group and they played until one o'clock in the morning.

Tuan: Sounds like you had a great time.

Lynn and Hoang were married last week. Use this model and talk about the ceremony and reception.

Lynn and Hoang arrived at the church.

1. arrive at the church

2. walk down the aisle

3. kiss
exchange rings

4. stop at a park
take photographs

5. arrive at the reception

6. have appetizers
drink

7. sit down
eat dinner

8. dance
talk

9. leave for their
honeymoon

57

Practice this model and ask questions about the pictures below.

> **What did he wear?**
>
> **He wore a tuxedo.**

1. What / wear?

2. When / arrive at the church?

3. Where / go on their honeymoon?

Partner Exercise

Student 1

What / the bride / wear?
What did the bride wear?

1. What / the bride / wear?
2. She / wear / a wedding gown
3. What / the groom / wear?
4. He / wear a tuxedo
5. How / bride / get to church?
6. She / come / in a limousine
7. What time / be / the wedding?
8. It / be / 4:00
9. How long / be / the wedding?
10. It / be / an hour.

(FOLD HERE)

Student 2

Listen carefully and help Student 1.

1. What did the bride wear?
2. She wore a wedding gown.
3. What did the groom wear?
4. He wore a tuxedo.
5. How did the bride get to church?
6. She came in a limousine.
7. What time was the wedding?
8. It was at 4:00.
9. How long was the wedding?
10. It was an hour.

Complete these questions and answers about the wedding reception.

1. Where ___**did they go**___ after the wedding?   To a park.
2. Why _____ there?   To take pictures.
3. What time _____ ?   It started at 5:00.
4. Where _____ ?   In a restaurant.
5. How many guests _____ ?   One hundred.
6. What _____ before dinner?   Appetizers and drinks.
7. What kind of music _____ ?   Slow music and rock.
8. Where _____ ?   To Hawaii.

In a small group, discuss these events. Answer the questions next to each picture.

Wedding

Did you ever attend a wedding in the United States?
Who got married?
Where was the wedding?
Where was the reception?
How many people attended the reception?
What did you eat?
What gift did you give to the couple?
Where did they go on their honeymoon?

Surprise Birthday Party

Did you ever attend a surprise birthday party in the United States?
How old was the person?
What time did the party begin?
What time did you arrive?
Was the person really surprised?
What gift did you bring?
What did you eat?
What did you do at the party?

Read and discuss the messages in the box below. Choose three appropriate greetings for each occasion and write them on the lines below.

Birthday

1. **You don't look a day over 25!**

   _____

2. _____

   _____

3. _____

   _____

Sickness

1. _____

2. _____

3. _____

Wedding

1. _____

2. _____

3. _____

Death

1. _____

2. _____

3. _____

---

1. With deepest sympathy on the loss of your mother
2. Hurry and get well
3. You don't look a day over 25!
4. For the two of you
5. You're not getting older, you're just getting better
6. We hope you're better soon
7. As you begin your life together . . .
8. May your faith bring you comfort
9. A special wish for a special person
10. Get well wishes from all of us
11. Our thoughts and prayers are with you
12. For both of you . . .

A FUNERAL

In the United States, funeral practices vary by religion and culture. Describe the funeral in the pictures below. Who attends each service? How is this funeral the same or different from funerals in your country? Use the vocabulary in the box to help you.

funeral home	minister / priest / rabbi	bury
deceased person	give a eulogy	grave
mourners	cemetery	tombstone
coffin	give condolences	say a prayer

. . .

wake / viewing	funeral service	burial

Sit in a small group. Discuss which services you would attend and the remembrance you would send for each situation below. Write your decisions on the chart.

1. What service would you attend?
    the wake
    the funeral service
    the burial

2. What would you send the family?
    a card
    flowers
    a fruit basket
    a contribution to charity
    money

DECEASED	I WOULD ATTEND	I WOULD SEND
A family member		
A friend		
A friend's mother		
A neighbor		
A co-worker		

11 Calling the Police

Discuss

Did you ever call the police?
Why did you call? What happened?
What are the telephone numbers for the
police, fire department, and rescue squad
in your area?

Read

The police department can help people to deal with many kinds of problems. You can call the police when you have a problem in your neighborhood, such as a robbery, a traffic accident, or neighbors who are fighting. Do not get involved in these incidents yourself. The police can also help in a medical emergency such as a heart attack, a poisoning, or a drowning. They can give first aid, call an ambulance, or provide any other necessary service.

In an emergency, call the police and tell them the problem and the location. For an accident, the police will ask if anyone is hurt. For a fire, the police will ask the type of fire. They will tell you to get everyone out of the house immediately. If someone is committing a serious crime, the police will tell you, "Stay on the line. Don't hang up." They will send a police car and continue to talk to you until they arrive. They will ask, "Where are you?"; "Can you see the person now?"; "Does he have a weapon?"

In some towns, the police emergency number is 911. In others, it is a local number. Look at your local police cars; the emergency number is in large print on the side. You should keep all emergency numbers near your telephone.

Read each sentence. If it is true, write T. If it is false, write F.

_____ 1. Call the police department if there is an automobile accident in your neighborhood.

_____ 2. Try to stop a fight between neighbors before you call the police.

_____ 3. Be sure to tell the exact location of a problem when you call the police.

_____ 4. If a man is trying to break into your house, the police will ask you to stay on the phone until they get there.

_____ 5. You should call the police if a child drank some household cleaner.

Police Operator:	Police Department.
Julia:	This is Julia Murray. There's a man breaking into my neighbor's apartment.
Police Operator:	The address?
Julia:	348 Collins Street.
Police Operator:	A patrol car is on the way. Stay on the line. Can you see him?
Julia:	Yes. He's climbing in the back window.

Practice this model with the following situations.

There **is a man breaking into my neighbor's apartment.**

1. a man / break into my neighbor's apartment

2. two men / fight in front of my house

3. a man / look in my window

4. two teenagers / throw rocks

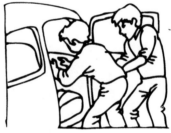

5. two boys / break into my car

6. some people / make a lot of noise upstairs

7. a teenager / rob a drugstore

8. a man / mug an old lady

9. a girl / scream for help

Partner Exercise

Student 1	Student 2
a man / break into my house There's a man breaking into my house.	*Listen carefully and help Student 1.*

Student 1

1. A man / break into my house

2. two women / sell drugs on the corner
3. two gangs / fight in the schoolyard
4. woman / scream for help

5. a man / beat his wife in the next apartment
6. a man / rob a gas station
7. a teenager / chase a boy down the street
8. a man / follow a child home

9. two boys / steal hubcaps from a car
10. some boys / race cars on my street

Student 2

Listen carefully and help Student 1.

1. There's a man breaking into my house.
2. There are two women selling drugs on the corner.
3. There are two gangs fighting in the schoolyard.
4. There's a woman screaming for help.
5. There's a man beating his wife in the next apartment.
6. There's a man robbing a gas station.
7. There's a teenager chasing a boy down the street.
8. There's a man following a child home.
9. There are two boys stealing hubcaps from a car.
10. There are some boys racing cars on my street.

(FOLD HERE)

Listen, Read and Say

Police Operator:	Police Operator.
Pierre:	A man just collapsed in the street. He's having a heart attack.
Police Operator:	Is he conscious?
Pierre:	Yes. His eyes are open, but he isn't moving.
Police Operator:	What's the location?
Pierre:	The corner of Henry Street and Atlantic Avenue.
Police Operator:	Your name?
Pierre:	Lester Pierre.
Police Operator:	We'll send an ambulance immediately.

Practice this model with the following situations.

> **A man** just *collapsed in the street.*
> **He's having a heart attack.**

64

1. A man / collapse in the street
   He / have a heart attack

2. Two boys / fall out of a boat
   They / drown

3. My son / swallow / a penny
   He / choke

4. My wife / fall down the stairs
   Her head / bleed

5. A dog / bite my son
   His arm / bleed

6. A bee / sting my daughter
   She / not breathe

7. My son / swallow some tranquilizers
   He / be unconscious

8. A car / crash into a tree
   The driver / lie on the street

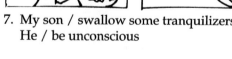    

9. A man / shoot my neighbor
   He / die

10. A young man / fall off a motorcycle
    He / be unconscious

Complete these telephone conversations between a police operator and a person calling to report an emergency.

Police: Police Department.

You: There _____

Police: What's the address?

You: _____

Police: We'll send someone immediately.

Police: Officer Shiffman.

You: A man just _____

Police: Is he conscious?

You: _____

Police: What's your location?

You: _____

Police: We're on our way.

Police: Police Dispatch.

You: _____

Police: The address?

You: _____

Police: A car is on the way.

Interaction

Ask two students these questions about an emergency they witnessed. Fill in their answers on the chart below.

Did you ever witness a crime or an emergency? What happened?
Who called the police? What did the police do?

	STUDENT 1	**STUDENT 2**
Situation		
Police Action		

Role play

With another student, write and practice a telephone conversation between a police officer and a witness to a crime or emergency. Explain the problem. Give the location and any other important information.

Michelle is a single parent with two young daughters, ages four and seven. She works as a waitress in a restaurant from 6:00 P.M. to 12 A.M. She doesn't have much money and is trying to support her two young children. She can't afford a baby sitter because it would cost her almost $100 a week. Every evening, she bathes the children, puts them in their pajamas, and reads them a story. Then she leaves them home alone. She says that they are fine and that they just fall asleep in front of the television. She puts them in bed when she gets home a little after midnight.

Discuss these questions.

1. How old are the children?
2. How do you think Michelle feels about leaving her children?
3. What might happen to the children while they are home alone?
4. What could Michelle do about her job and her children?
5. Would you call the police if Michelle lived next to you?
6. What would you do if Michelle lived next door to you? Write your opinion below. Share your opinion with the other students.

_____

_____

_____

12 Crime

Discuss

Were you ever mugged or robbed?
What happened?
Did you ever have to describe a suspect to
the police?

Read

If you are the victim of a crime or see a crime, report it to the police immediately. Call the police in the town in which the crime occurs, not the town you live in. When the police arrive, they will first take care of the emergency or crime. They will then speak with the victim and the people who witnessed the incident.

The officer will ask you to describe carefully the person or people you saw. Try to remember as many details as you can. Was the person tall or short, heavy or thin, young or old? Was there anything special about his appearance, voice, or hair style? Did he use a name? Look at the person's clothes and remember the color and style.

Other details are also important. If there was a car, look at the license plate first. Then try to remember the color, the make, or special features. Write down these details if possible. Look at your watch and remember the exact time. The more information you can give to the police, the faster they can find and arrest the suspect.

In serious crimes, the police may ask you to come to the police station and look at photographs. Or they may ask you to identify a suspect in a police line-up. In a police line-up, several people stand in a special room; you can see them, but they can't see you. If you are the victim of a serious crime or witness a violent crime, you may need to appear in court. However, in most cases, a court appearance is not necessary.

Read each sentence. If it is true, write T. If it is false, write F.

_____ 1. Give only the important details when you report an incident to the police.

_____ 2. Special features of a suspect, such as a beard or a scar, are very helpful to the police.

_____ 3. The license plate number is the most important information you can give the police about the car.

_____ 4. If you witness a crime, you have to identify the suspect in a police line-up.

_____ 5. If you point to a suspect in a police line-up, he can see you.

Mrs. Ortiz: I was mugged! A teenager stole my pocketbook and my watch.
Policeman: Can you describe him?
Mrs. Ortiz: Him? It was a girl! She was white, about 17 years old. She was about 5' 6" tall and very thin.
Policeman: What about her hair?
Mrs. Ortiz: She had long brown hair.
Policeman: What was she wearing?
Mrs. Ortiz: She was wearing blue jeans and a yellow top.
Policeman: Was there anything special about her?
Mrs. Ortiz: I can't remember anything special.

Practice this model with the pictures below.

I was mugged!
A ___***man hit***___ me and ***grabbed my gold chain.***

1. hit / grab my gold chain

2. push / run off with my pocketbook

3. shoot / take my wallet

4. stab / steal my money

Practice this model with the descriptions below.

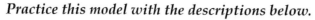

| A: Can you describe ___**him**___ ? | A: Can you describe ___**him**___ ? |
| B: ___**He**___ was **Caucasian**. | B: ___**He**___ had **a moustache**. |

1. Caucasian
   white

2. Afro-American
   black

3. Latino
   Hispanic

4. Asian-American
   oriental

5. young

6. middle-aged

7. short

8. average height

9. tall

10. thin

11. average weight

12. heavy

13. a moustache

14. a beard

15. a scar

16. a tattoo

17. straight hair

18. wavy hair

19. curly hair

20. long black hair

Describe each suspect.

Student 1

He / oriental
He was oriental.

1. He / oriental
2. He / about thirty years old
3. He / an accent
4. He / bald
5. She / young
6. She / long black hair
7. She / black
8. She / a tattoo on her hand
9. He / white
10. He / a beard
11. His hair / average length
12. He / a scar on his cheek

(FOLD HERE)

Student 2
Listen carefully and help Student 1.

1. He was oriental.
2. He was about thirty years old.
3. He had an accent.
4. He was bald.
5. She was young.
6. She had long black hair.
7. She was black.
8. She had a tattoo on her hand.
9. He was white.
10. He had a beard.
11. His hair was average length.
12. He had a scar on his cheek.

Look at these two suspects carefully. Fill in their descriptions in the sentences below.

He was _____.
    (race)

He was _____.
    (age)

He was _____ and _____.
    (height)   (weight)

He had _____ hair.
    (length)   (type)

It was _____.
    (color)

He had a _____.
            (special feature)

He was wearing _____

    and _____.

She was _____.
    (race)

She was _____.
    (age)

She was _____ and _____.
    (height)   (weight)

She had _____ hair.
    (length)   (type)

It was _____.
    (color)

She had a _____.
            (special feature)

She was wearing _____

    and _____.

You are a witness to a serious crime. The victim is in the hospital and will recover. The police are asking any witnesses to come forward with any information they have about the crime. If you call or go to the police station and say that you witnessed the crime, you know that you will need to go through photographs and identify the suspect in a line-up. There is a very small possibility that you will need to go to court.

Discuss these questions.

1. Describe the crime.
2. Describe the mugger.
3. Is the woman resisting or is she letting him take her pocketbook?
4. Where is the witness?
5. If you are a witness, what will the police ask you to do?
6. What would you do if you witnessed this crime? Write your opinion below. Share your ideas with the other students.

_____

_____

_____

This is the young man who robbed a woman outside your apartment building last week. Complete the information in the boxes.

IN CASE OF CRIME
CALL THE POLICE IMMEDIATELY
FILL IN THE BOXES

SEX	RACE	AGE	HEIGHT	WEIGHT

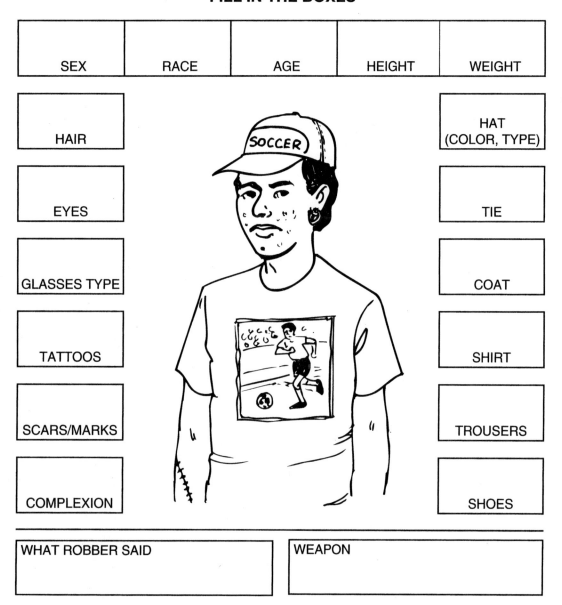

HAIR

EYES

GLASSES TYPE

TATTOOS

SCARS/MARKS

COMPLEXION

HAT
(COLOR, TYPE)

TIE

COAT

SHIRT

TROUSERS

SHOES

WHAT ROBBER SAID

WEAPON

Role play

With another student, write and practice a conversation between an investigating officer and the victim of a crime. Describe the crime and the robber. The officer will ask for exact details about the robber's description and actions. Present your dialogue to the class.

73

13 Work

Discuss

What did you do in your country?
Where are you working now?
What kind of job would you like in this country?

Read

There are many job opportunities in the United States. However, it is not easy to find a job. To find a job that you like, you need to match your previous work experience, education, and interests with the jobs in your area.

Develop a realistic job plan for yourself. What skills do you have? What is your educational background? How well do you speak English? What do you like to do? Do you like to work with people or work alone? Can you go to school full time or do you have to work and go to school part time?

For example, a student may decide to be an accountant because she enjoys working with numbers and working in an independent atmosphere. It may take from six to eight years to learn English and get the necessary credentials at a college to become an accountant. The student might first consider a short-term training program to get an entry-level job as a data entry clerk. While working, she can continue to learn more English and take accounting and business courses at a college. After two or three years, she might get a job as a bookkeeper. Then, she can continue on the accountant career ladder to junior accountant and finally accountant.

A vocational counselor at your school can give you information about jobs and training programs at vocational schools, community colleges, and four-year colleges in your area. Some vocational and trade schools are very expensive. Before registering for these schools, it is important to speak to former students and a counselor to be sure it is the right program for you.

Read each sentence. If it is true, write T. If it is false, write F.

_____ 1. It is easy to find a good-paying job in the United States.

_____ 2. It can take a long time to reach your career goals.

_____ 3. While you are studying, it is a good idea to find an entry-level job in the career area you want.

_____ 4. All vocational and trade schools can help you reach your job goals.

_____ 5. It is realistic to work full time and study full time.

Counselor: From our conversation last week, you seem to like to help people and enjoy physical activity.

Laura: Yes, I like to work with other people.

Counselor: You've also expressed an interest in the health field. One job you might consider is a nurse's aide.

Laura: What does a nurse's aide do?

Counselor: A nurse's aide works in a hospital or a nursing home and does general patient care. For example, a nurse's aide makes beds, feeds and washes patients, and takes patients for walks.

Laura: I think I'd like that. Could you tell me more about the requirements?

Counselor: Sure.

Practice this model with the responsibilities of a nurse's aide.

A nurse's aide ___*changes beds.*___

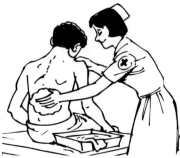

1. change beds

2. dress and undress patients

3. feed patients

4. bathe patients

5. empty bedpans

6. take and record temperatures

7. record liquid intake and output

8. answer call lights

9. transport patients in wheelchairs

Sit in a small group. Discuss the job responsibilities for each of the jobs below. Then, write the number of the job on the line in front of each responsibility.

1. bookkeeper

2. medical lab assistant

3. heating and cooling technician

4. security guard

2	Performs lab tests and reports results
_____	Guards an employer's property to prevent theft or damage
_____	Installs air-conditioning and heating units
_____	Analyzes and records financial transactions
_____	Checks the identity of individuals entering a building
_____	Maintains payroll and account records, using computer programs
_____	Cleans and sterilizes lab equipment
_____	Tests and fixes heating and refrigeration units
_____	Uses hand and power tools
_____	Answers questions about customers' accounts
_____	Monitors surveillance equipment
_____	Prepares and mails out bills to customers
_____	Conducts investigations about accidents or crimes

Complete this information about your job.

Where do you work? _____

What do you do? _____

What are the responsibilities of your job? _____

_____

_____

Sit in a small group. Discuss the characteristics a person should have for each of the jobs below. Then, write the number of the job on the line in front of each characteristic.

1. bank teller

2. practical nurse

3. cook
   food service worker

4. electronic and communication
   technician

2	Be able to understand medical terminology
_____	Be able to count and make change accurately
_____	Be able to read recipes and food orders accurately
_____	Be able to read and understand technical manuals
_____	Be able to test and analyze electronic equipment with accuracy
_____	Be able to work with kitchen equipment
_____	Be able to communicate with patients
_____	Be able to work with customers quickly and courteously
_____	Be able to tolerate high temperatures and humidity
_____	Be able to follow policies and procedures in care of patients
_____	Be able to solve technical problems
_____	Be able to assemble parts and equipment
_____	Have a good sense of taste and smell
_____	Have a desire to work with people who are ill
_____	Have physical ability to work with patients and equipment

What are the characteristics of your job?

_____

_____

_____

Read and discuss the educational requirements for the jobs below. Then, ask another student the questions about his or her job interests.

Job	Educational Requirements
Nurse's Aide	High school diploma + on-the-job hospital training or short vocational program
Bookkeeper	High school diploma + vocational program or some college courses
Medical Lab Assistant	High school diploma + certificate from vocational program or community college
Heating and Cooling Technician	High school diploma + apprenticeship or vocational program
Security Guard	High school diploma preferred
Bank Teller	High school diploma + on-the-job-training
Cook / Food Service Worker	High school diploma preferred, vocational programs available
Practical Nurse	High school diploma + license from a one-year (full-time) program at community college or hospital
Electronics Technician	High school diploma + one-to-two year vocational or community college program

Ask another student these questions about one of the jobs above or another job he or she is interested in. Fill in the chart below with information about your partner and about yourself.

	YOUR PARTNER	YOU
What is your job experience?		
What job are you interested in for the future?		
Why would you choose that job?		
How long will it take you to reach your goal? Why?		

Sherry works part time as a home health aide. She's an intermediate ESL student at her local adult school. Next month Sherry will begin her on-the-job training project as a nurse's aide at General Hospital. She will work full time and continue to take ESL courses. As soon as she finishes her ESL program, she will begin an LPN program at the local community college. It takes one year full time to get an LPN license, but Sherry will take two or three years to complete the program part time. Her long-range goal is to become a registered nurse. RN programs require from two to three years of full-time study. Sherry knows that this opportunity may be several years in the future, but believes that she has developed a realistic plan.

| home health aide | nurse's aide | licensed practical nurse | registered nurse |

Discuss these questions.

1. Where is Sherry going to take the nurse's aide program?
2. How long does it take to complete an LPN program full time?
3. Why will it take Sherry more than one year to complete her LPN program?
4. What difficulties might Sherry have while she is in the LPN program?
5. What is Sherry's career goal?
6. How many years from now do you expect her to get her RN license?
7. Why might it be difficult for her to become an RN?
8. What should she do in order to reach her long-range goal?

 **Go FIND OUT** *What are some job training programs at vocational schools, trade schools, and community colleges in your area? Visit a job-training program and talk with a counselor. Bring in any information, brochures, or catalogs and share them with the class.*

 What are your long-range career plans? Why are you interested in that job? How do you plan to reach your goals?

14 Benefits

Discuss

Are you working?
What benefits do you have?
What deductions are taken out of your paycheck?

Read

When you are looking for a job, you should consider the salary and the job benefits. Benefits usually include medical insurance, vacation and sick days, and pension plans. Some jobs have very good benefits, while others do not have any.

The most important benefit is medical insurance. Some businesses give medical insurance benefits that pay for doctors and hospitals, while other companies only give hospital coverage. Most businesses or unions give employees either family or individual coverage. In some medical insurance plans, employees have to pay a yearly deductible and a percentage of doctor fees. Sometimes, employees pay a fee to join a group of doctors, called a Health Maintenance Organization (HMO), in which most medical services in the group are free. Prescription, dental, and eyeglass plans are also available to many employees through their companies or unions.

If you are choosing between two jobs, look at both the salary and the benefit package. Family medical insurance is very expensive. If one job pays $30,000 but has no benefits and the second job pays $26,000 but offers good medical insurance and other benefits, the second might be a better salary.

Read each sentence. If it is true, write T. If it is false, write F.

_____ 1. All companies give medical insurance to their employees.

_____ 2. Medical insurance plans from work always cover the employee and the employee's family.

_____ 3. Employees never have to pay for job benefits.

_____ 4. Most medical insurance plans are the same.

_____ 5. When comparing two jobs, benefits are sometimes more important than the salary.

Listen, Read and Say

Mike: Did you get your raise?

Brian: Yes, but I'm not taking home much more money.

Mike: I can't believe how much they withhold from my paycheck each week.

Brian: Yeah. It's difficult to make ends meet every month.

Mike: You said it! I had to pick up an extra job on Saturdays.

Brian: My wife went back to work part time and I try to work as much overtime as possible.

Mike: I hope things get better soon.

Practice
Practice

Talk about this paycheck with the sentences below.

Brian Cho		153-42-6321		Dependents: 2		6/06–6/12
EARNINGS				**WITHHOLDING**		
Type	Rate	Hours	Amount	Type	Amount	YTD Amount
Regular	8.15	40	326.00	SOC SEC	23.05	645.40
Overtime	12.22	4.5	54.99	MEDICARE	5.39	150.92
				FEDERAL	40.90	1145.20
				STATE	7.44	208.32
	Total		371.99	DBL/SUI	1.86	52.08
Total Withholding			106.59	UNION	1.92	53.76
	Net pay		265.40	PENSION	18.59	520.52
	Total	YTD	10,398.22	HEALTH	7.44	208.32

Brian's gross pay is $_____.

Brian's take-home pay is $_____ a week.
 net pay

He earns $ _____ per hour.

He earns $ _____ per hour overtime.

Brian worked _____ hours overtime last week.

Brian claims _____ dependents.

Payroll takes out $_____ for _____.

                              federal taxes
                              state taxes
                              social security taxes
                              medicare
                              pension
                              union dues
                              a credit union loan
                              medical insurance
                              disability and SUI
                                  (State Unemployment Insurance)

So far this year, Brian has earned $_____.

Talk about Susan's benefits with this model. Then talk about your own benefits.

Susan has _**health insurance.**_
Susan doesn't have _**dental coverage.**_

I have _**health insurance.**_
I don't have _**dental coverage.**_

1. health insurance

2. dental coverage

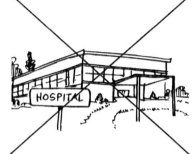

3. hospital insurance

4. a prescription plan

5. eyeglass coverage

6. life insurance

7. ten vacation days

8. four sick days

9. personal days

10. educational benefits

11. discounts on purchases

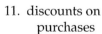

12. a pension plan

Complete these sentences about the benefits you receive from work.

1. I *have / don't have* medical insurance. My insurance covers about _____% of a visit to the doctor.

2. I *have / don't have* a prescription plan. Each prescription costs me

   _____.

3. I *have / don't have* a pension plan. I contribute _____ each paycheck; my company contributes _____.

4. I get _____ personal days. Last year, I used them to _____

   _____.

5. I get _____ sick days. Last year, I was out _____ days. So far this year, I have used _____ sick days.

6. I *have / don't have* dental insurance. My insurance covers about _____% of each visit to the dentist.

7. My company *offers / doesn't offer* educational benefits. If I go to school, they pay *all / part* of the tuition.

8. I get _____ vacation days. After I work at the company for _____ more years, I will get _____ vacation days.

9. My company also has a life insurance policy for me for $_____.

10. I *receive / don't receive* special discounts from my company.

    For example, _____.

Interaction

Ask two students who are working if they receive benefits. If the answer is "yes," ask for more information. Fill in the chart below.

Do you have _____?

BENEFIT	STUDENT 1	STUDENT 2
health insurance		
dental insurance		
vacation days		
sick days		
personal days		
a pension plan		
special benefits		
educational benefits		

Brian has good benefits at his job. He gets medical insurance, disability, and a pension. Answer the following questions about his benefits.

DOCTOR	HOSPITAL	DISABILITY	PENSION
•80% of costs up to $5,000 •100% of costs over $5,000 •$400 deductible	•100% of cost for 1–120 days •No deductible	•Short term = full pay •Long term (over six months) = 60% of salary	•Company contributes 4% •Employee contributes 5% •Employee can retire at 60 with 30 years on the job

1. For doctor bills, how much is the deductible for the year?
2. What percentage does Brian's insurance pay for each doctor's visit?
3. How long can he stay in the hospital with no charge?
4. How long will he get full pay if he has to go on disability?
5. How much does Brian's company contribute to his pension plan?
6. How much does he contribute to his pension plan?
7. Does he have dental or eyeglass coverage?

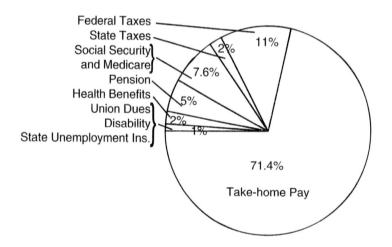

1. What percentage of Brian's check is withheld for federal taxes?
2. What percentage of the check is withheld for the union, disability, and state unemployment insurance altogether?
3. What percentage of the check is take-home pay?
4. What is the total percentage of the check that is withheld?

Sit in a small group. Figure out these math problems about paychecks.

1. Jack makes $6.75 an hour. He works 35 hours a week. How much does he make a week?

2. Last week Barbara worked 43 hours. She makes $6.60 for the first 40 hours and $9.75 for every hour over 40 hours. How much did she make altogether?

3. Last week Karen made $520 before taxes. She worked 40 hours. How much did she make an hour?

4. David earns $6.00 per hour for his regular salary. If he works overtime, he earns 1 1/2 times his regular hourly rate. How much does he make an hour for overtime?

5. Josh's gross pay is $1,152.62 every two weeks. His take-home pay is $796.68. How much do they withhold from his paycheck every two weeks?

6. Bill will make $7.35 an hour the first six months on his job. He will then receive a $.45 an hour raise after the first six months if his performance is good. He will receive another $.35 raise after one year on the job. What will his salary per hour be after one year?

7. Kim earns $489 a week. How much does she make yearly?

15 Telephone

Discuss

Were you ever late for work? For an appointment? For any other commitment? Did you call to say you would be late? What excuse did you give?

Read

Americans always expect a telephone call if someone is going to be late, absent from work, or is not able to keep an appointment. You must always give the reason why you cannot come or why you will be late.

If you have to be late or absent from your job, you must call your employer as early as possible and tell her the reason. There are very few acceptable excuses: you are sick, you have a family emergency, or you have a transportation problem. It is often better to say "I have a personal emergency" instead of giving details of a family problem. For example, you might not want to tell your boss that you had to talk to your son's teacher because he got into a fight at school yesterday. If you're going to be late for work, say what time you plan to arrive. If you're going to be absent, tell when you will return to work. It is never a good idea to be late for work. Frequent late arrivals are a problem, no matter what the excuse.

Read each sentence. If it is true, write T. If it is false, write F.

_____ 1. You are expected to arrive on time for all business and personal appointments.

_____ 2. If you miss your train and you are going to be an hour late for work, call from the train station.

_____ 3. Getting new tires for your car is an acceptable excuse to be absent from work.

_____ 4. A death in your immediate family is an acceptable excuse to be absent from work.

_____ 5. If you are late once a month, you may lose your job.

Secretary:	Atlas Corporation.
Mrs. Dole:	This is Mary Dole. May I speak to Mrs. Johnson, please?
Secretary:	Mrs. Johnson is out of the office now. Can I take a message?
Mrs. Dole:	Please tell her that I'll be late for work today. My car broke down. I'll be in at 10:00.
Secretary:	I'll tell her as soon as she returns.
Mrs. Dole:	Thank you.

Practice
Practice

Practice this model with the excuses below.

I'll be late for ____**work**____ because
____**my car broke down.**____

1. work
   car / break down

2. the meeting
   have a flat tire

3. the appointment
   the train / come late

4. work
   have an emergency

5. the interview
   get lost

6. school
   miss the bus

Call and give the reason that you will be late.

Student 1

I / work / miss the bus
I'll be late for work because I missed the bus.

1. I / work / miss the bus

2. I / the appointment / my car break down

3. I / the interview / have an emergency at home

4. I / the meeting / the bus be late

5. I / work / have a flat tire

6. I / the interview / get stuck in traffic

7. I / work / have a minor accident

8. I / my appointment / my babysitter come late

9. My daughter / school / oversleep

10. My son / school / have dentist appointment

(FOLD HERE)

Student 2
Listen carefully and help Student 1.

1. I'll be late for work because I missed the bus.

2. I'll be late for the appointment because my car broke down.

3. I'll be late for the interview because I had an emergency at home.

4. I'll be late for the meeting because the bus was late.

5. I'll be late for work because I had a flat tire.

6. I'll be late for the interview because I got stuck in traffic.

7. I'll be late for work because I had a minor accident.

8. I'll be late for my appointment because my babysitter came late.

9. My daughter will be late for school because she overslept.

10. My son will be late for school because he had a dentist appointment.

Practice

Practice this model with the information below. Use the name of a friend.

Please tell _____ **Sue** _____ that I won't be able to _**go shopping**_ because I have to _**wait for the plumber.**_

1. go shopping

wait for plumber

2. come over

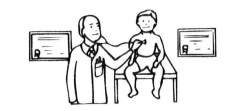

take my son to the doctor

3. take him to work

visit my _____

4. pick her up

work overtime

5. meet him

drive my _____ to school

Complete these telephone conversations. Use your own name and give an excuse.

1. A: Sweet Tooth Bakery.

   B: Hi, Gail. This is _____. Can I speak to Bob?

   A: Bob's with a customer right now. Can I take a message?

   B: Please tell _____ that _____ late for work because

   _____.

   A: I'll tell _____ as soon as _____ finishes.

2. A: Hi. This is _____. Is Jenny there?

   B: Sorry. _____ out right now.

   A: Could you please tell _____ that I _____

   because _____.

   B: Sure. I'll tell her.

3. A: Eastern Electronics.

   B: This is _____. May I speak with Carolyn Moran?

   A: _____ out to lunch now. Can I take a message?

   B: Please tell _____ that _____ late for my interview because

   _____.

   A: Yes. I'll give _____ the message.

Interaction

Ask two students these questions about calling in late for work or school. Fill in their answers on the chart below.

	STUDENT 1	STUDENT 2
Were you ever late for work? For school? For an appointment?		
Did you call?		
Who(m) did you speak to?		
What excuse did you give?		

Sit in a small group. You are going to be late for work. Read and discuss each excuse below. If it is acceptable, check "Yes." If it is not acceptable, check "No."

		Yes	No
1.	I have a dentist appointment.	____	____
2.	I have to drive my children to school this morning.	____	____
3.	I have a personal emergency.	____	____
4.	My car won't start.	____	____
5.	I overslept.	____	____
6.	My boiler is broken. I have to wait for the plumber.	____	____
7.	I have to speak to my son's teacher.	____	____
8.	My child is sick.	____	____
9.	The babysitter didn't come yet.	____	____
10.	I have to take my child to the doctor.	____	____

Role play

With another student, write and practice a conversation between an employee and a boss. Explain that you will be late for work and give a reason. Present your dialogue to the class.

Mary's brother, Paul, was supposed to arrive at the airport on Saturday morning, but he came a day early. Mary is ready to leave for work. She just received Paul's call. He's waiting for her at the airport, which is about thirty minutes from her home.

Discuss these questions.

1. Where is Paul?
2. Where is he traveling from? Do you think he speaks English?
3. How does he feel?
4. Why is Mary upset?
5. Where do you think she works?
6. Do you think it will be easy for her to take off from work or to come late to work today?

Sit in a small group and discuss these questions. Write your answers below. Then, share your answers with other groups in the class.

1. What are Mary's options? What could she do?

   She could _____

   She could _____

2. If Mary decides to pick up her brother, when should she call her boss?

   She should _____

3. If Mary decides to pick up her brother, what should she tell her boss?

   She should _____